SCREEN GODDESSES

SCREEN GODDESSES

Tom Hutchinson

This edition produced exclusively for

WH SMITH

Dedicated to my own family Pantheon:
Pat and Michael and Stephen with tyro-goddess
Janetta having her own special Porsche-shaped,
plush-lined niche. Ming-Chui Benjamin, too.

Photographic acknowledgments
All photographs in this book are from The Kobal
Collection, London, with the exception of the
following:
Euro Collection, London, pages 123, 125, 187.

Front cover: Claudette Colbert in *Cleopatra*, 1934
              (Kobal Collection, London)
Back cover: Portrait of Brigitte Bardot (Kobal
              Collection, London)
Title page: *Cover Girl*, 1944 (Kobal Collection,
              London)

This edition produced exclusively for
W H Smith

Published by
Deans International Publishing
52–54 Southwark Street, London SE1 1UA
A division of The Hamlyn Publishing Group Limited
London · New York · Sydney · Toronto

Copyright © The Hamlyn Publishing Group Limited 1984
ISBN 0 603 03576 0

Printed in Italy

Contents

A Pantheon of Primitives

In the beginning was the Bird, by which I mean Woman in the London Cockney-vernacular sense. But it takes on a literal meaning in a non-sexist manner that would not disgrace those feminist descendants of Aristophanes' 'Lysistrata' down to Mrs Emmeline Pankhurst and the turned-again Germaine Greer.

The Bird I am talking about is a high-flier, seemingly unattainable by the base lusts and desires of mere men; above the

Meek and Mild, Mother and Child. Theda Bara in uncharacteristic haloed pose in Heart And Soul *(1917).*

stresses and strains of sexuality – and yet responding to, and sustained by, the currents of those needs. The Feminine Principle is what transforms the idea of Woman into a goddess; and in art that Principle has always been necessary: an idealization devoutly to be wished. It became an idolization in which women in turn began to believe – an immaculacy embodied within the concept of a Virgin Mary.

Because of the original mystery of Woman's ability to bring life into the world, the female sex took on an honour tinged with terror for the poor masculine mutts who went out to forage for food outside the camp-fire glow of domesticity and calm. Cave-drawings show women with cooking utensils or standing with mysterious intent in profile to reveal bellies ballooning with pregnancy. Food and sex were necessities for continued existence. Man, as is his nature, made holy virtues out of that necessity.

A whole machinery of myth, of which women were a necessary part, was thus set in motion; from the Egyptians via the Celts to the Ancient Greeks, whose gods were more human than human in that their marriages, infidelities and quirks of character mimicked so eloquently the domestic sit-coms of mortal human beings.

As civilization assumed its identity, so the Church in its various denominations knew a good thing when it saw it, realizing that while the Virgin Mary could be deified almost as much as the Son of Man – not the Son of Woman, you understand – Mariolatry should not give women ideas above their station. The fact of their sex was a trap and a snare, because they were the cause of Original Sin – the Bird had become in D.H. Lawrence's terms, a Plumed Serpent. And, while women were cherished for their frailties, they were also regarded as

May MacAvoy in A Private Scandal *(1921). Note the crucifix – holiness was always next to sexiness.*

creatures who could the most easily fall into the Devil's grasp – and drag men with them.

Women, while publicly disliking this idea, could yet use it as a means to an end, powers behind and on various thrones, as in the case of the Borgias, or they could use the simple fact of their fragile femininity to conquer prejudice mercilessly, as did the first Queen Elizabeth. But on the stage, which might have been thought the natural platform for a woman to show off all her enticements and allures, women were kept at bay for a long time – with boys cosmeticizing their faces to play female roles. This situation could not over-long endure and eventually what had been called a monstrous regiment of women – by a divine obviously influenced by that notorious sexist St. Paul – broke ranks to assume its rightful place on the stage.

The placing of Woman on a pedestal had, you might say if you were so cynically minded, two other subconscious reasons besides the obvious one of adoration in the Arthurian sense (one of those legends that both had its flesh and ate it by regarding Guinevere as both holy Queen and unfaithful whore). Set high on a pedestal the Woman was thus out of the fray of dealing with day-to-day life and could have no positive control or sway over it. And, being on a pedestal, made it all the easier for men to peer circumspectly up her skirts, all the better to try to glimpse that tender trap which man-created religion had warned them about.

It is, for instance, a notable fact that, in the late nineteenth century, never were so many brothels opened, nor so much pornography displayed while the port was being passed in men-only parlours, al-

Erich von Stroheim had a number of film fetishes – but he did like women to be fin de siècle. *Here's Mae Murray in his* The Merry Widow (*MGM, 1925*).

though women – following Queen Victoria's self-effacing lead – were swathed with clothes and swaddled with circumstance.

By coming down into the arena of showbusiness, women could be seen for the first time as human beings and as partners with men – albeit still passive ones – in their appreciation of sex and the ways of the world. And as men were made into stage gods via the loud approbation of their audiences, so women were turned into goddesses. It was, perhaps, inevitable that as the twentieth century dawned the Feminine Principle in showbusiness terms was roughly and vaguely associated with the Victorian concept of 'The Mother' and 'The Whore' – the Mother idea covered the girl-next-door species, while the Whore was a generous cloak covering those aspects of femininity that might be considered

straight-speaking, if not necessarily loose-living. In the American theatre, for instance, there was Amelia Bingham, forever cast in the role of Mother Nature in some improbable but smug allegory, while Louise Lester, of similarly ample proportions stood holding between two podgy fingers the mark of possible immorality – a lighted cigarette.

It is an intriguing comment, also, upon the fancies of the turn-of-the-century urban male that the theatre of this time should have had such a preponderance of plays, extravaganzas and musicals devoted to the Far East where, in harems of singularly tatty allure, women were at their most submissive and pliant, without a voice in their own destinies. Other productions of a popular nature – such as melodramas of the Old Red Barn type – were concerned with women for whom Virtue was the highest

honour for which a Woman could and should die without endangering her enshrined virginity.

Then along came movies .... Showbusiness gods and goddesses, so far only partially haloed for chosen audiences on stage, were at last limelit for the masses. The Pantheon was now rigged so high that millions of people all over the world could see what was writ there. And on the screen, for all to see, were their own desires, fears and loves looming large and made holy by magnitude. It was the human personality shining through that made those actors and actresses into gods and goddesses; the Female Principle had won through.

Early Heroines and Goddesses

Hollywood was a place that was scarcely mentioned as a location, if at all, in school text-books, even in America. (It is still more a state of mind than a geographical situation.) But it was here that the infant movie industry began to rear its multifaceted head. While *The Great Train Robbery* (1903) might prove, with its story of male-only skulduggery, that women were not necessary to such a tale of urgency and tension, women and girls were arriving on the cinema scene in all shapes and sizes. It is notable that the great director, D.W. Griffith's first movie, *The Adventures of Dollie* (1908), which was less than one reel in length, concerned the progress and plight of a female, in this case a little girl. The girl is kidnapped by gypsies and concealed in a barrel. This drops off a gypsy waggon as it fords a river and is swept downstream and over a waterfall, smashing to reveal the girl-child inside ready to be picked up into the loving arms of her anxious, distraught father. (Griffith was later,

Warming herself at the fire-glow and at the glow of public approval. Bessie Love photographed by Abbee – in Paris, of course.

interestingly enough, to expand, adapt and elaborate this simple theme into some complex tensions which take on the role of great cinematic art; though, in later cases, Man is able to interrupt and halt the flow of Nature's malevolence by way of his courage.)

Also in 1908, Griffith made another short movie called *The Fatal Hour* which was about the always topical white-slave traffic made so relevant an issue in the grey lives of people by the yellow press. Here Oriental white-slavers kidnapped girls in New York and transported them to New Jersey. The movie concentrates on one spunky lass who, in the final scene is tied up in a hut, affixed to a revolver which, in turn, is connected to a clock – which will detonate the gun at the appropriate moment.

The following year Griffith made *Her Terrible Ordeal* which had the heroine trapped in the bank-safe over a weekend in which suffocation would seem about to be her principal method of relaxation. In *The Girl And Her Trust* (1912) a notable transformation took place. The girl herself became a minor heroine, not relying on others for alleviation of her ordeal. She is a telegraphist holding off thieves who take her aboard their getaway vehicle – a railroad car.

D.W. Griffith made these movies for the Biograph Company, before going on to form his own studios. And it was the public who made such companies aware that their unpublicized stars were worthy of more prominence. In other words it was the public who demanded the star-system.

Domestic strife or a domestic wife? Mrs. Jones Entertains was made by D.W. Griffith in 1909 (American Mutoscope and Biograph).

The masked avengers?
Title of this was 'A Gay
Biograph Party'.

Thus, in 1908, after a mounting flood of letters from picturegoers and exhibitors asking who she was, Florence Lawrence was revealed as 'The Biograph Girl'. She had been spotted in many, many Biograph one-reelers, but because the Company had never thought to announce her name on the films – perhaps for fear that she might want more money from her meagre contract – she was virtually anonymous.

She had had some stage experience, but her quality of imp-like personality was of such potency that fans became inquisitive, wanting to put a name to the person who was part of their entertainment. Florence Lawrence was soon to be forgotten among

the spate of new faces that surged upon the screen as though in response to this public need to adore and identify. And little enough is known of her or her history. But she can, to some credible degree, be noted as one of the first stars of the cinema – if not *the* first star. Certainly, she was the first acknowledged goddess.

Now that we have returned to the word goddess, how to define it? My dictionary calls it a female deity ruling over some aspect of the universe and/or of human life; a beautiful or much-loved woman. The latter definition implies, of course, the way we regard screen goddesses. And it is one of the remarkable facts that such goddesses were

primarily supposed to be above the battle of the sexes. Women adored such deities just as much as men; they were, for them, creatures to be admired and emulated in the hope that by touching the hem of such a garment of holiness, the disease of frustrated ordinariness might be alleviated. For instance, Mary Pickford and her little-girl look had as many if not more women admirers as men. To that extent such goddesses were asexual, although their private lives might bring them down to the earth of ordinary humanity with a satisfyingly salacious bump.

But in elevating its own goddesses, the film industry first tried to utilize those goddesses who had already been made in other spheres, such as actresses who had achieved a high reputation on stage. Thus Sarah Bernhardt – 'the Divine Sarah' as she was known – deigned to make a French film, *Queen Elizabeth*, notable for its sumptuous costumes if not for the resplendence of its acting. A vast legend on stage, it was unfortunate for her that sound had not been invented because that reputation on stage had been greatly enhanced by accounts of the quality of her voice – 'which could range over all the cadences of human passion, thrilling the audience to an ecstasy of belief in the characters so portrayed'. Some of her most successful roles had, in fact, been of men, and so remarkable was her talent that it was said to have been almost unapparent that she had only one leg – her right leg was amputated in 1915 after an accident.

Queen Elizabeth was very much of a certain style of movie in those days. While Griffith was exploring ways of moving the camera and helping to create the ways of cinema, many other movies were of a stately mien which marked them out as owing principal allegiance to the theatre and its prosceniums. So, in paying tribute to a woman who had become a goddess in real life, the film of *Cleopatra* (1912) was so static as to seem retarded. It starred actress Helen Gardner in what has been called the biggest asp-disaster in the world, and it was told in a series of posed tableaux interspersed with lengthy and complicated narrative-titles. It ran for just under sixty minutes and, despite Miss Gardner's physical eloquence – it might even be called rant-

Below: Sarah Bernhardt just had to get into the act. Here she's emoting in a slow, turgid version of Queen Elizabeth *(Histrionic Film, 1912).*

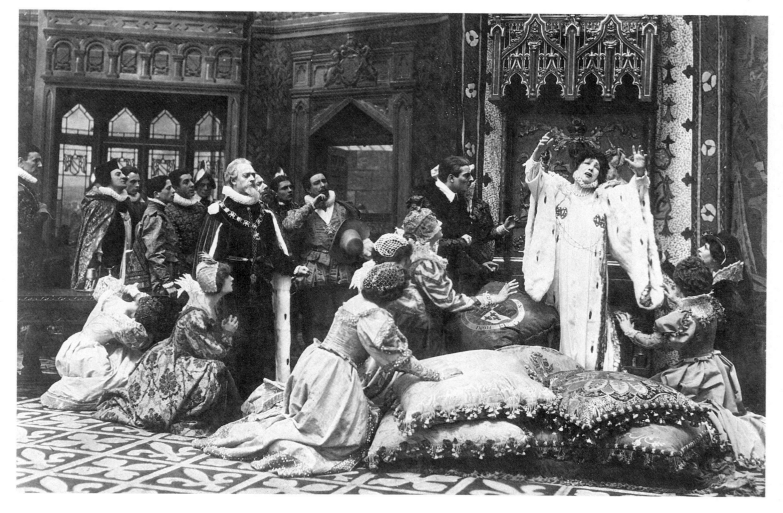

13

ing – seems even longer. This is not the patronizing sneer of hindsight; even at the time people thought it slow, while its spectacle was really a faint echo of the realistic display then apparent in the plays being exhibited on New York City's Broadway and London's West End. Such filmed theatre did little to help propel the infant art of cinema on its way, but it was a stage – literally – that had to be gone through,

before much else could be achieved.

It is an intriguing thought that artistic nourishment was to come not from that which was deemed aesthetically high, such as the theatre, but from the peep-show origins that might well be thought to pander to an audience's undoubted appetite for salacity. The white-slave traffic, therefore, came in for a good deal of footage, but in many of these so-called pot-boilers could be

this story, though a synopsis indicates that women here were not treated so much as goddesses as tarnished angels – besmirched by the machinations of wicked men. How close were films to the Victorian ethos!

The Vamp

Gradually the Feminine Principle, through all the movies made in those early days before, during and after the First World War, polarized into two very distinct attitudes for and on behalf of women; the Whore and the Mother became ideals refracted into other, more assimilable goddess-blueprints: the Vamp and the Little Girl. Theda Bara and Mary Pickford. Both were to attract many imitators for their distinctive and contrasting styles of presentation in the vehicles made to exhibit them, and Theda Bara's reign as The Vamp was to last only a short while. But their two-pronged influence was to be long-lasting and to impose on future goddesses an approach instantly recognizable to future audiences.

Brigitte Bardot is in direct line of succession to Theda Bara as 'the woman who did not care' while Mary Pickford's pre-Lolita cocky innocence has its descendants in the vulnerability of, say, a Shirley MacLaine or a Barbra Streisand (as in the transvestite *Yentl*).

The lure of the Orient, and the attraction – sexual, that is – of Egypt had been indicated by Helen Gardner's Cleopatra, so it was inevitable that Theda Bara would herself play Cleopatra in the film of that name in 1917. Even by that time her screen image had become the kind of woman that the real Cleopatra was supposed to be in the popular imagination. She was not only a snare and a delusion for the male, but she also actually enjoyed entrapping him and, so it was implied, she might well have enjoyed the sexual possession. Women's suffrage was not, by any means at this time, a universal right but here was a woman who voted with her body – electing herself tempter and tyrant at one and the same time.

Theda Bara was, as is well known, a publicist's fable, her name anagramatically implying all the hidden voluptuousness that Rudolph Valentino in *The Sheik* would similarly enjoy in public favour. For Theda Bara read 'Arab Death' equating the sins of the flesh with the judgment that would surely come for such transgression – if all

felt a narrative-drive and an urgency which owed more, thankfully, to gutter-journalism than the upper echelons of received good taste. Such a film was *Traffic In Souls* (1913), a supposed exposé of white slavery which was said – so the publicity had it – to have been made without the knowing consent of the studio front-office which might have been appalled by the nature of the product. Little has survived of

Opposite: *Theda Bara again, and you might just detect behind all the publicized make-up the face of a little girl lost.*

flesh was grass, what a ripe reaping would be made on the Day of Retribution!

Theda Bara's allure today seems so alien as to inspire ridicule that it could ever have been considered sexually attractive: the eyes and lips etched in charcoal to make her face resemble a doll-like automaton; the hands and body usually in a posture which, to our view, would seem about as seductive as a slumped sack. Yet, as the historian David Thomson has written: 'She was the first woman offered commercially, in movies, as an object of sexual fantasy.' In 1914 William Fox had bought the film rights to the stage play, 'A Fool There Was' and its director, Frank Powell, found Theda Bara to play the vamp.

Her real name was, in fact, Theodosia Goodman, a mouthful of verbiage to put up on a marquee, especially as her role in cinematic life was to be a badwoman .... Yet, as several writers have pointed out, there was no other performer who was so well known in such a brief space of time,

Right: *Abandon hope, O, mortal man! Such abandonment is once more from* Cleopatra *with Theda Bara (Fox, 1917).*

apart from Valentino and Mae West. She was, in short, a superstar within a few months of the release of the film in the early months of 1915. She was a goddess, even if her emotions were deemed to be those of the nether regions, rather than from the upper emotional air which goddesses are primarily supposed to breathe.

The stage play of 'A Fool There Was' had been evoked by a poem by Rudyard Kipling, 'The Vampire' which – it was said – had been evoked by a painting from the pre-Raphaelite, Philip Burne-Jones. The Vamp was not an original creation; the Danish actress Betty Nansen had already portrayed her and her wilful ways. So, too, had Virginia Pearson, who had taken on the role on stage. She, though – perhaps fearing type-casting – turned down the chance of re-creating the part on film, as did Alice Hollister who had already appeared in a film called *The Vampire* – a similar story about a similar woman. In horror stories such a personification would have been called a succubus, but these stories had less to do with the supernatural than the natural facts of love and lust.

Miss Goodman had appeared in a small

Theda Bara casting an oriental spell once more in The Soul Of Buddha *(1918). The orient and sex were strangely synonymous in the public mind.*

role in a minor film called *The Stain* under her stage name of Theodosia de Coppet and she accepted the role in *A Fool There Was* for $100 a week – a low amount even then. Her earnings were to rise remarkably, for the public fell for the idea of The Vamp and the name of Theda Bara was invented.

Theda Bara is an example of how a goddess can be made not born, for a journalist called Al Selig was put in charge of building up her image, of publicizing her as though she were already a legend in her own vamptime. 'De Bara' had been the name of her grandmother and Theda was her family's affectionate shortening of Theodosia. But the twist-around of 'Arab Death' sounded much more in keeping with the kind of atmosphere that Selig and his assistants wanted to activate. The stories rose to skyscraper storeys of fantasy to convince a willing public that they were being let in on one of the secrets of the age.

One of the most popular of these publicity tales was that Theda was the daughter of a French artist and his Arabian mistress and was born under the shadow of the Sphinx, which gave her occult powers. The interest in the occult was considerable at about this time – the First World War nourished the belief that there might be life after such intolerable and massive death – and that, too, helped along the Theda Bara legend.

So her kohl-rimmed eyes – weary beyond the fatigue of supposedly mortal women – became a mascara-fad among the many women who thronged to see her films. For it was not only the males who fell victim to her power. Despite the overt movements of her sexual progress there could be also sensed a feeling that all flesh and love could be enjoyed, whatever its nature or gender. Whether sublimated or not there is, even in Theda Bara, a certain androgynous quality which was to be refracted and made even more evident in other goddesses who were to come. She was a *femme* not only *fatale* to men but to women. She implied the untold conspiracy that women felt at about this time regarding a masculinity that had been so obviously dominant for so long.

Newspaper and magazine journalists seized upon her for human, or rather inhuman, interest stories, one such reporting how sad it was to be Theda Bara in the real world. She told him: 'As I was walking near my home I had a great big red apple in my hand and ahead of me I spied a little girl with thin legs and, oh, such a hungry look. I put

A bridal Bara? Here our Theda is a nurse who falls lustfully in love with a young divinity student – but through that love she finds redemption. From When A Woman Sins *(1918).*

Not the dance of the seven veils but a strenuous scene from Salome *(1918) with Theda Bara, unnamed lady – and knife.*

my arms around her and put the apple in her hand. Her eyes fell on my face and a look of terror came into hers. "It's the Vampire!" She ran . . . and I went home and sobbed like the littlest child.' The lot of a netherworld goddess could indeed be unhappy, but there was always the money – and growing fame, even if some civic dignitaries declined to meet her on publicity tours, for fear that their high office would be tainted by contact.

Miss Goodman was not, it must be said, totally averse to the morbidity of this hype. Louella Parsons, the gossip columnist, then establishing some reputation, reported in her column about a press conference: 'She received us in a darkened parlour, draped with black and red, in the tones of her sweep-ing gown. She was white, languid and poisonously polite. The air was heavy with tuberoses and incense. The staging worked magic. The interviews were in hushed tones and the results were columns. When the door closed on the last caller the windows went up. "Give me air!" she commanded.' *La Belle Dame Sans Merci* was here being revved up by twentieth-century publicity; the two made a remarkable combination.

Theda Bara took sex seriously at a time when it was hardly mentioned as being taken at all. She made some historical spectacles and movies, which did not have her vamping along with an expectant audience, but she was primarily known as The Vamp and that was the way she was forever to be hype-cast as well as type-cast.

The film historian John Kobal noted that she made forty films in her three years at Fox Studios, but only *A Fool There Was* seems to have survived. In a way the paucity of visual information about her seems to give her another kind of allure; in her movies she was notorious for being ferociously and aggressively approachable; in real life she was – albeit, unconsciously – distant and remote because of that lack of what we know about her. Despite several attempts at comebacks she, in fact, retired in 1919 having married Charles Brabin, director of some of her movies. Kobal noted that, when she died in 1955, she was still married to him – 'and, in that, she was probably unique as well.'

She was, in her way, the female equivalent of Valentino, whose sweeping ways with women were to make him an idol with feet made of only too human clay. For him, as for Theda, human life and love were very much a gland affair, both of them at the mercy – in cinematic terms, at least – of sexual urges beyond their control. There were other vamps, as I have indicated, but looking through old photographs of them they seem pale imitations of the lustrously pallid original. Seena Owen, Valeska Surat, Luise Glaum . . . the glamour was in the rapacity of their appetite for men and sensation, even if it was punished later. But they come nowhere near Theda in star quality – or, at any rate, the star quality that was so much evidenced in public approbation.

She was, in her dynamic way, a counterblast to the 'good' girls of the screen, from Lillian Gish via Mae Marsh to Bessie Love, and of course Mary Pickford.

Theda herself realized this, that she was riding high on a gimmick which was a reaction *against* rather than a *raison d'être*: 'I like the adventuress because she has colour and intensity . . . . She is the only human sort of woman the American public wants. They must have colourless heroines or sugar-sweet heroines playing white little parts in white little love stories. I am not saying that American women are like that; they are warm, wonderful vital things, but people seem to want heroines and not women. Therefore, I choose to play wicked women, because when photoplay women are good and real they often cease to be women.'

There is here, it must be admitted, a lively appreciation of the kind of mould into which the public – and, especially, Americans – wanted their film-women to be cast. There is, again, the mood of The Mother and The Whore, a quality made more concrete because of the pioneer nature of early America when there was all the difference between a woman who wanted to look after her menfolk and the waggon-train groupies who were just along for the ride – and the money to be obtained from the next saloon.

Good Girls

Lillian Gish and her sister Dorothy were – despite the imposed gentility of their times and type-casting – lucky to have secured the attention of D.W. Griffith, a director who was one of the first geniuses of the cinema. For him Lillian made such classics as *Way Down East* and to him she accorded the worship that today seems quaint and yet rather touching. Even in later years she was wont to call him 'Mr. Griffith' as though to call him by his first name would have been *lèse majesté* of the worst and most distasteful kind.

One of the most remarkable and satisfying films that Lillian made for Griffith was *Orphans Of The Storm* (1921), along with her sister Dorothy. Based on a popular play, '*Les Deux Orphelines*' about the French Revolution it contained some spectacular crowd scenes re-creating eighteenth-century Paris and revealed Lillian in one of her most famous postures – that of misunderstood and martyred woman, for whom life seems one vast frame-up.

There was here, as in many of Griffith's films, a strong tinge of Charles Dickens, especially in the way that heroines were always so naive, innocent and almost at times, risible. For instance, Lillian is thrown into prison on a false charge but for Griffith it was the greater evil that she was a 'fallen woman' when she was sent to prison. It becomes a fairly blunt point of morality for that to be a consideration . . . .

A great director of the silent cinema, Erich von Stroheim, once told me: 'D.W. had a strange relationship with the Gish sisters; although he bullied them mercilessly while they were on the film set he regarded what they represented on screen as being of the finest and purest and most holy. His relationship with them was of the highest in private life; of that I have no doubt. But he saw in them, in Lillian es-

MOTION PICTURE

DECEMBER - 25 CTS

A BREWSTER MAGAZINE

Lillian Gish

As the movies waxed lyrical about their women, so fan magazines used them as cover come-ons for ever-hungry addicts of the screen.

pecially, an unattainability which he translated into his movies. I once said to him: "D.W., I believe that if you could you would have Lillian play Christ." And he looked at me as though I had read his innermost thoughts.'

It is often felt that D.W. Griffith was only a master of pure and spectacular epics, such as *Intolerance*, and this synopsis for *Orphans Of The Storm* surely reveals this: 'Scenes are shown of the exaggerated luxury of those last days, of the tottering omnipotence of the monarchy. The orgies and tyrannies of a section of the old French aristocracy are shown as they affect the common people . . . it shows more vividly than any book of history can tell that the tyranny of kings and nobles is hard to bear, but that the tyranny of the mob under blood-lusting rulers is intolerable.'

Yet Griffith realized, as do many great artists, that the general does not communicate as emotionally as the particular. The individual is always the easier to identify with – rather than the crowd. And the woman individual is even easier. Thus, Gish . . . .

The way that she and Dorothy made their way into the cinema is itself a fairy-tale of its kind. Born De Guiche in Springfield, Ohio, and deserted by their father at an early age – in Griffith they undoubtedly found a father-figure – the girls went to visit their friend Mary Pickford at Biograph Studios, were seen by Griffith and teased and coaxed into films. That was *An Unseen Enemy* (1912) and many others followed for Griffith, including *The Birth of A Nation* (1915) and *An Innocent Magdalene* (1916). In 1916 she was also the girl rocking the cradle of humanity in his *Intolerance*.

Her spinsterish innocence was not only a fact of her commercial life, selling purity to a public that, actually, was becoming jaded with it in the 1920s, but a fact of her personal life. It is reported, for instance, that after signing later with MGM for six films, studio boss Irving Thalberg urged her to participate in some sort of scandal. Perhaps her image would then be more easily assimilated by a box-office that was becoming more and more aware of flappers and a general air of sexual laxity which would have made the guilty sinfulness of a Theda Bara even more laughable and which was, paradoxically, also considered to be counter to Lillian's obvious and general demeanour. This had a pre-Raphaelite quality that transmuted even the most sin-besotted character into a symbol of some sort of virginity . . . . Lillian Gish steadfastly refused Thalberg's offer of an arranged scandal, on the same style as an arranged marriage, and her career gradually faded.

Femininity triumphant in the persons of Mary Pickford and Lillian Gish, in the centre, and Dorothy Gish on the right. But who the girls are on the extreme left and behind remains a mystery.

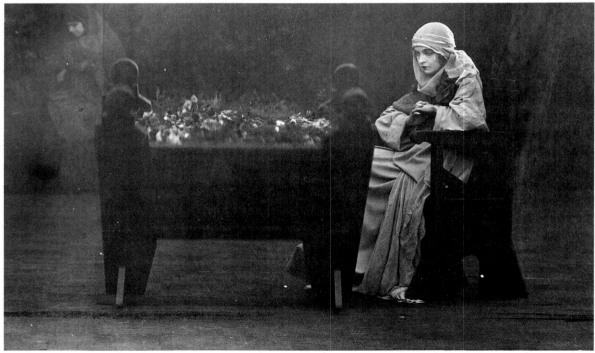

Above: A scene from the heart-rending Broken Blossoms *with Lillian Gish approaching very timidly her cruel father, played by Donald Crisp (D.W. Griffith, 1919).*

Right: Lillian Gish's is the hand rocking the cradle of the world in Intolerance *(D.W. Griffith, 1916).*

Paris during the Revolution created by D.W. Griffith for Orphans Of The Storm *(1921).*

It was, though, restored for a small time by her remarkable appearance as a grandmother-figure defending two children against the evil of their stepfather, Robert Mitchum in Charles Laughton's *The Night Of The Hunter* (1955). Here was her early austere innocence brought up to date – and packing a powerful punch as well as shotgun.

All the actresses of that time – including the Vamps – had, seen from the cynical hindsight of today, *sweet* faces. They had an innocence there, perhaps because their faces were so new to an industry which was itself new to itself. Their faces had not grown calloused and experienced with knowledge of themselves and others, and the limelight had not had time to tan the features with its own brand of sophistication. It was there as well in the attitude towards films, because movies were, in

Mid-western minds, anyway, the nearest thing to white-slavery that a gal might know . . . unless she was very careful.

The ingenue Bessie Love was another young innocent taken on board by D.W. Griffith. He once told her she was lucky, because of his studio's artistic integrity, not to have gone to a cheaper studio and been ruined. Bessie looked at him, eyes widening, and said that she knew all about those poor, *ruined* girls. D.W. Griffith looked at her hard, realized she wasn't joking and snorted amicably: 'Oh, I didn't mean *that*!'

She portrayed the Bride of Cana in the Judean episode of Griffith's *Intolerance*. She herself has recounted what making films could mean to the people of that time, how during the Trial of Jesus Lillian Gish was so perturbed by the cries of 'Crucify Him' that she burst into tears and had to leave the filming to compose herself. Born Juanita

27

Horton in Midland, Texas, Bessie had entered films in 1915 while she was still a pupil at a Los Angeles high school. Her own career switchbacked from being a sweet-sixteener to a serious leading lady. But it never quite took off and consolidated into anything that was firm in the public imagination. Perhaps there were too many girls like her around in those early days . . . she has described the kind of charm school that D.W. Griffith originated where poise, posture and proper walking were taught. She was taught singing, which she supposed was to develop her chest.

There was even a 'den-mother,' Mrs. Lucille Brown, to attend to the morality and look to the health of the girls. Bessie remembered one statement above all others, as she was being groomed to be a goddess, and it was about the distance between the human being that hides behind the mask of deity and the image portrayed.

Said Griffith: 'Never meet your film favourites. You'll only be disappointed.'

It was obvious that in those days Bessie was being assembled into one of the many imitations of Mary Pickford, the original World's Sweetheart. Such films as *Nina The Flower Girl* (1916) with its blatant use of sentimentality – a poor girl lost amid the jungle of high society – were typical of those movies. So was *A Daughter of The Poor* (1917) which again showed the lot of the poverty-struck girl bent on trying to preserve her innocence in a world which seemed dedicated to removing it.

She was, though, always much more interesting as a screen personality when she was no longer going through the emotional wringer of those roles. She was, later, to appear as a drug-crazed girl in *Human Wreckage* (1918) and was to bring a modicum of jokiness to coping with dinosaurs in the first movie of Sir Arthur

Opposite: Richard Barthelmess and Lillian Gish in D.W. Griffith's Way Down East *(1920), a melodrama as moving as it was powerful*

Below: A jollier time was being had by all in See America Thirst *(1930) with Bessie Love the centre of attention from Slim Summerville (left) and Harry Langdon (right).*

Conan Doyle's 'The Lost World.' In that she even managed to up-stage – if only for a time – a monkey called Jocko.

But, basically, in her early days, she was considered, along with so many others, to be a Pickford look-alike. While she was making *Nina The Flower Girl* she recalled that the director Lloyd Ingraham, despite his swear-words, always treated her as a child and wanted her to imitate Mary Pickford in the way she was to hold herself.

Pickford

Mary Pickford, there is no question, dominated the era – despite the Vamps and all the others. Mary Pickford once visited London with her recently married partner Douglas Fairbanks, whose athleticism had triumphed as her communicated naïvety had similarly flourished. They were, in that union, mated above and beyond the idea of mere royalty to a kind of godhead. Mary Pickford looked through the window and

From America's sweetheart to the world's sweetheart and one of her most popular roles in Rebecca Of Sunnybrook Farm *(TCF 1938).*

saw the worshippers below: 'Outside the window we saw them, thousands and thousands of them, waiting day and night in the streets below, just for a glimpse of us.' While Fairbanks accentuated the positive, Pickford had similarly eliminated the negative in her own screen characterizations. The result was an alarming combination of potent magic.

She had been born Gladys Smith in Toronto and her father was killed when she was five. (It is interesting how many silent women stars were without fathers, either through divorce or death.) She toured with several stock companies through the USA and Canada and became known as Little Gladys, her halo of golden curls giving her an instant and recognizable identity. She charmed actor-manager David Belasco into giving her a role in serious theatre – she was only thirteen – and, similarly, won over D.W. Griffith who was then at Biograph.

The actors and actresses who worked for these companies were, as I have said, unidentified, but Little Mary – Belasco had changed her name – soon became known throughout the world. After that, Mary Pickford, the child-woman elevated to the power of goddess, was very much 'The World's Sweetheart.' In an age before Lolita it is hard to realize why there was such an attraction about her which appealed to the public. Perhaps it was because she embodied the spirit of both Peter Pan and Wendy – the vulnerable truculence of Peter and the sweet mothering of Wendy.

In 1923 Mary Pickford appealed, through the fan-magazine 'Photoplay,' for ideas about which parts she might play, roles which would give her greater scope for her talents. The answers included Cinderella, Heidi, Alice from Wonderland and Through the Looking Glass, Anne of Green Gables . . . the public loved her in those

little-girl-lost-and-found characterizations and, perhaps wearily, she acceded to their requests (or, rather demands) playing Little Mary way into her twenties and beyond.

She made seventy-five two-reelers for Griffith at Biograph, but she was, it seems, annoyed by Griffith's discovery of Mae Marsh as another queen-bee and so left. She was a harder businesswoman than most of the other silent screen goddesses – those days of being mother's helper to a bereft family had paid off in an ability to read small print – and, in 1919, she formed United Artists with Charles Chaplin, D.W. Griffith and Douglas Fairbanks. She was ruthless enough where money was concerned. She had married Fairbanks – after a marriage to Owen Moore – but it was obvious that she yearned for movies to take her out of the Pollyanna rut of *Daddy Long Legs* (1919) and *Little Lord Fauntleroy*

(1920). So much so that she brought over the German director Ernst Lubitsch in 1923, perhaps hoping that he would view her in a different light. He did, in *The Parade's Gone By* (1923) and *Rosita* (1923), but the public was not at all happy with this new sophistication that was laid upon their Little Mary. And, neither, it is possible was she. Anyway, she soon reverted to *Dorothy Vernon of Haddon Hall* (1924) and *Little Annie Rooney* (1925). The titles tell all.

One of the side-issues affected by this public determination that Mary should stay adolescent was that camera lighting had to suggest that Mary was forever youthful and cameraman Charles Rosher – her favourite – has said that he innovated many ideas because it was essential to keep her looking young. Mary Pickford was still playing little-girl roles way past the age of thirty and it is a tribute to her own spectacular spirit – and to the work of her lighting camera-

Douglas Fairbanks Senior, Charlie Chaplin and Mary Pickford off on a U.S. bond-selling tour during the First World War. Stars were expected to put their time and talents into the war effort.

33

men – that the face which was her fortune should have survived so long in the public esteem. Basically, she retired from movie acting in 1933 – perhaps sound tolled her knell as well – after winning an Oscar for *Coquette* in 1929. As though that retirement marked the passing of another kind of era, she and Fairbanks were divorced in 1936. She married Charles 'Buddy' Rogers in 1937 and became a recluse, putting money occasionally into the production of other people's films and being given another, Special, Oscar in 1975. She died in 1979.

Silence had been golden for Mary Pickford; it had also been amazingly constricting, casting her forever in roles that – in later years – she confessed that she would rather not have played.

May McAvoy

But women were breaking out of the corsetting that audiences demanded of their goddesses, just as the flappers were confining their breasts to suggest a unisexuality that might appear to put them on a par with men after universal suffrage had been announced. An actress, such as May McAvoy, could move from the *The Enchanted Cottage* (1924) to a dinosaur epic, such as *The Savage* (1926), and also appear in the mammoth *Ben Hur* (1926). Variety was the spice not only of her life, but her film contract.

Miss McAvoy is not one of the most lustrous and luminous names in the history of early films, but she was a hard-working professional who did her acting chores with a minimum of fuss and a modicum of res-

Mary Pickford being allowed to look her age for once as Dorothy Vernon Of Haddon Hall *(1924). Period clothes suited her, she said.*

A severely posed still from Mary Pickford's Coquette *(1929). A toast without wine-glasses?*

pect for her craft. Her role in *The Enchanted Cottage* – Sir Arthur Wing Pinero's fantasy about the maimed young officer who suddenly sees the plain girl he married as a beauty – is still very touching. A review at the time said: 'The change in May McAvoy as Laura Pennington is far more striking. First she is seen with protruding teeth, tired eyes circled with wrinkles and a prominent nose. There is nothing farcical about her countenance; she is merely unprepossessing. In a second or so the plain face fades out, its place being taken by one with even teeth, pretty lips and a modest and straight little nose. It is almost incredible that May McAvoy, an actress of undeniable beauty, could be so different with a set of false teeth and a bump on her nose.'

False teeth, though, do not an actress make nor a nose-bump the kind of professional that May McAvoy was. She was born to wealth in New York City and the sense of money behind her allowed her to make decisions and defy orders when other less secure actresses might well have given in for the sake of opportunity. The

35

American poet Carl Sandburg called her 'a star-eyed goddess' which was enough to send any girl reeling at the time and she was of a temperament spirited enough to refuse to accede to Cecil B. De Mille's suggestion that she appear scantily clad in his *Adam's Rib* (1923). Such defiance did not seem to do her career much harm as a working goddess. For Lubitsch she played in Oscar Wilde's *Lady Windermere's Fan* and in 1926 was the beloved Esther to Ramon Navarro's Prince of Hur in *Ben Hur*. The posters swooned on about: 'The Inspired Love Of The Prince Of Hur For The Gentle, Lovely Esther.' In later years she was to recall that during the making of this monumental movie – costing $6,000,000 – she narrowly escaped severe injury when a set burst into flame while she was standing on it talking to someone whose conversation so enraptured her that she was hardly aware, at first, that sparks were flying upwards.

She was conscious only of the sparks of his words. Her fellow conversationalist was F. Scott Fitzgerald, chronicler of the Jazz Age through which they were both journeying.

It is an irony of the kind that gives fate a bad name for its only-too-glaring coincidences that the film that was to usher out the cinema's Silent Age was also to be called *The Jazz Singer* (1927) and was to star not only Al Jolson but May McAvoy herself. It would seem that jazz had a great deal to do with Miss McAvoy's life.

Sexual Preferences

Then, as now, there were directors with preferences for one or the other sex – in terms of cinematic manipulation only, let it be added. Just as George Cukor was to become famous in later years for his ability to cope with such 'difficult' stars as Katharine Hepburn, so D.W. Griffith en-

Opposite: May McAvoy in The Enchanted Cottage *(1924) – to prove that love is blind.*

Below: Oscar Wilde's Lady Windermere's Fan *(Warner 1925). Note the woman's appearance, halfway between temptress and haute couture.*

Woman as comforter. Mary McAvoy consoles Al Jolson in The Jazz Singer, *perhaps telling him he can get that make-up off (Warner 1927).*

joyed directing women in his epics. For instance, when Douglas Fairbanks emigrated from the New York stage he worked for Griffith at Triangle Studios. For Fairbanks, who was to become one of the really immense stars of the silent screen – marriage to Mary Pickford only consolidated that reputation – it was the fulfilment of a dream. He had always wanted to work with Griffith, and, as he wrote: 'I never spent any evening more thrilling, entertaining or instructional than when I saw *Birth Of A Nation*. I went four or five nights, one after the other. Till then I had never thought of going into films.'

But Griffith, who was much more concerned with building up the Gish sisters, was to disillusion him. He 'buried Fairbanks in lack-lustre make-up which almost negated him' for a film called *The Lamb* and then hardly spoke a word to him. It was a woman, though, who helped rescue Fairbanks from anonymity, a fate worse than death for any actor. This was Anita Loos, the scriptwriter, who later wrote *Gentlemen Prefer Blondes*, and she and director John Emerson put Fairbanks into a series of comedy-romances which allowed his breezy manner to shine through like a water-mark.

The appeal of Fairbanks was robust and vigorous, well in keeping with his much-publicized motto, 'Never Say Die!' and his oft-proclaimed ability to do all his own stunts in the adventure films which were to be his true *métier*. 'Laugh at your work and make it easy, start the day with a smile, the greatest thing in this little old world is enthusiasm ... have that unconquerable spirit of enterprise that laughs at reverses, takes obstacles as something to whet the appetite for further endeavours and fights for what it wants for the pure joy of fighting ....' In the land of Dale Carnegie such simplistic notions must have seemed heaven-sent; certainly he became the most popular of all the great cinema athletes.

He and Mary Pickford appeared in films together, notably *The Taming Of The Shrew*, yet her little-girl image seemed rather incongruous when set beside his blusteringly happy machismo.

'The Girl with the Bee-Stung Lips'

More in keeping with the Fairbanks' style would have been Mae Murray who was said to 'think of all the things a girl would not do in real life and then goes ahead and does them.' She was, in fact, a girl of limited acting ability yet her personality was so assembled by her studio, and the directors she worked with, that she became a top money-making star of the kind only films could have created.

She had a facial beauty that astonished, accentuated by lips which made the publicists describe her as 'The Girl With The Bee-Stung Lips'. They seemed always set in a provocative pout, inviting masculine collision. She seemed not so much the girl next door as the girl from the night-club down the road.

She was born Marie Adrienne Koening, the daughter of Austrian and Belgian

Here's woman as shrew in Taming Of The Shrew. *Mary Pickford and Douglas Fairbanks senior. As a variation of Shakespeare it had its moments (United Artists/ Pickford/Elton 1929).*

A prototype Marlene Dietrich? Directed by Josef von Sternberg, this had Mae Murray enwrapped with Basil Rathbone in The Masked Bride *(1925).*

immigrants, and her dancing ability brought her to Broadway where she became Vernon Castle's partner for a time. Her dancing in fact may well have accounted for her sinuous and inviting posture; she had the sexiest slouch in the business. She was glamorously blonde and the plots of her films are best described as 'madly improbable'. Parents may have railed against her strange coiffeurs and bizarrely-revealing clothes, but she was marvellously imitable for young fans who were feeling their way towards an identity and freedom in the age of flappers.

Some of Mae Murray's better movies were directed by Robert Z. Leonard, her third husband, but her finest hour and role came with *The Merry Widow*, directed by Erich von Stroheim. He had more patience than a similar authoritarian master, Josef von Sternberg, who after a few days working with her on *The Masked Bride* walked off the set – and didn't come back.

She appeared with some of the best male stars of the time, including Valentino and John Gilbert, and her career might have had no decline but for her fourth marriage, to Prince David Mdivani, who managed her affairs. Her popularity certainly helped MGM Studios to tide over its financial affairs which had been considerably tattered by stockmarket events. She and MGM thus had a mutual admiration society going. But the Prince insisted that she walk out of her MGM contract – the reason why is obscure, despite a good deal of documentation in other directions – and even after she found great difficulty in getting other roles. Hollywood could be a merciless nay-sayer when it felt that one of its great powers had been wronged.

Occasionally the name of Mae Murray would appear once again in headlines – sadly in connection with some symptom of her decline, such as bankruptcy – and in 1959 she wrote her autobiography which was called 'The Self-Enchanted'. But for a time in the days when silence was golden in the cinema, it had been she who had enchanted others . . . .

Where would The Merry Widow *be without a waltz? Here it is with Mae Murray yearning away under the bright lights (MGM 1925).*

Although she said she was never an official Sennett bathing beauty, Gloria Swanson was in Keystone comedies such as this with Bobby Vernon.

La Swanson

It was said of Gloria Swanson that she appeared in movies much like those of Mae Murray's – silly, extravagant and absurd – but unlike Mae Murray, La Swanson had a real acting sense and talent and could mock those swooning roles of sensual abandonment with a delicious sense of humour which an audience could readily appreciate. She was also possessed of a glamour which millions of American women admired – it was a question of dress-sense and the way she looked. And she pursued her ambition to be a great star with ruthlessness, from rigorous exercises to her fabled vegetarian diet.

She was of Swedish-Italian descent and, as a young teenager, visited Chicago's Essanay Studios in 1913 where she was taken on as an extra and met the actor Wallace Beery whom she married in 1916. In her autobiography her wedding-night encounter with Beery is still described with loathing. It did not, however, diminish her appreciation for the celebration of marriage, as she wed for the sixth time in 1976.

She had worked, in the early years, with Mack Sennett at Keystone, but although she posed as one of his bathing beauties she was never really one of them. As she told me in her later years: 'I couldn't even swim.' Not that that would have mattered, because Sennett's beauties were of the kind whose bathing suits rarely got wet – decoration was the name of their game.

She starred, after initial comedies, in a series of lachrymose dramas for Cecil B. De

Mille and then, financed by Joseph P. Kennedy, father of the late President, she embarked on *Queen Kelly* which Erich von Stroheim was to direct. He got only a little way into the movie, because she became increasingly irritated by the way he was turning a romantic melodrama into what would seem to be a series of appendices for inclusion in the work of Krafft-Ebing – aberration was the name of von Stroheim's game. But it was a game that Swanson wanted none of – she valued her public image almost as much as the public itself – and von Stroheim never completed the film, although a version prepared by Gloria Swanson was released.

Ironically, a small scene from *Queen Kelly* appears in the film that made Gloria Swanson famous for the second time around, *Sunset Boulevard* (1950) in which she played the retired, hysterical movie star clutching onto the chance of new fame and an even newer lover in the shape of William Holden. Both von Stroheim (as her butler) and De Mille (as her old director) appeared in *Sunset Boulevard*. Old scores had obviously been forgotten and old sores healed.

She was a consummate show-woman for her silent-era time. Even her marriage – her third – to a real-life French marquis seems now to be a gesture as manipulative as it was flamboyant. 'Arrange procession!' she is said to have cabled her film studio about her arrival from France with her new husband (the Marquis de la Falaise).

Cecil B. de Mille specialized early on in movies of lush sexual implication. Gloria Swanson here looks pained by it all in The Affairs Of Anatol *(De Mille-Paramount, 1921).*

For all that seeming contrivance, though, she was doubtless a warm-hearted goddess of some loyalty. She adored Sennett and, for instance, made nine films with the same director, Sam Wood: *The Impossible Mrs. Bellew* (1922), *My American Wife* (1922) and *Bluebeard's Eighth Wife* (1923) among them.

Despite their lurid titles they were, as movies, considerably better than the De Mille dramas which were at once hypocritical and slightly smutty: *Male And Female* (1919), *The Affairs Of Anatol* (1921) . . . . 'De Mille directs as though he believed everyone was carrying a dirty postcard in his pocket or handbag; there is a prurience about his work which no amount of whitewash can hide.' The writer of that was talking about De Mille's version of *Cleopatra*, but he might well have been writing about this series of movies.

Another director with whom she was much associated was Allan Dwan, again over quite a few movies, such as *A Society Scandal* (1924) and *Wages Of Virtue* (1924). She was very loyal to those she liked and even those whose work she had come to dislike, such as von Stroheim.

A European Goddess

In terms of high-class glamour few goddesses equalled Gloria Swanson, although Pola Negri ran her a close second. She, too, was *soignée* to the point of men's distraction; one had the feeling that only the whitest of silk sheets would ever grace the bed to which her eyes were constantly luring men. She had what Americans believed to be a European understanding of her femininity, which is as it should be because Pola Negri – born Barbara Appolonia Chapulek – was from Europe and

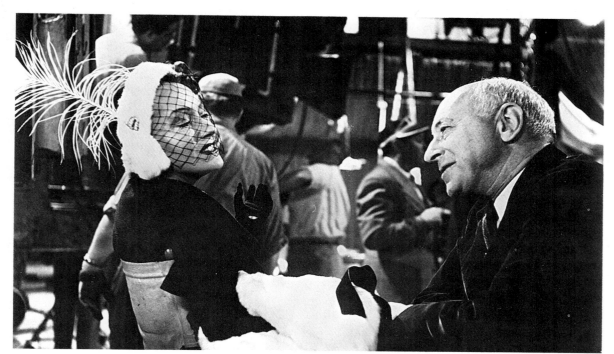

was the first European actress to be brought to Hollywood. Her rivalry to Swanson was fuelled by the studios in the hope that the publicity would enhance her reputation.

In fact it needed little enhancing, for Negri was a natural presence on screen. Coincidentally, she had married the brother of the Prince Mdvani, who had wed Mae Murray for a disastrous time; and before that she had married the Polish Count Dambski and so she was a real-life Countess. The films she had made in Europe caused Charles Chaplin, who had met her in Germany, to say that she was the 'greatest emotional actress and woman in Europe'.

Her arrival in Hollywood did not meet with a fanfare of approval from other actresses, who were reported in the fan magazines to have been more than a little disdainful of this woman who was supposed to be going to teach them how to project sex. Her contract was with Paramount whose idea of sophistication was to put her into a film called *Bella Donna* (1923), whose title tells all about the *femme fatale* she was supposed to be. Pola Negri was then placed in other films that tried to exploit her sense of the tragic side of sexuality, such as *The Cheat* (1923), and *Shadows of Paris* (1924). But it was only with Ernst Lubitsch that she achieved any kind of *rapport* with her cinematic material, with *Forbidden Paradise* (1924).

Her *forte* was the world-weariness that comes to women who have lives that have been much lived-in and loved-in. For instance, *The Woman From Moscow* (1928) had her – and I quote the publicity blurb – as 'a woman who took an oath. She swore she would find the man who has killed her fiancé. She swore to avenge his death.' Despite all this swearing, however, when she found the man she couldn't go through with her threat. This shows you couldn't trust a world-weary woman, such as Negri, to finish what she set out to do.

Her film temperament was, basically, a heavy one. She was an instinctive actress whose leaning was towards the tragic and her roles in Europe had been of that very nature. But Hollywood did not know how to treat that quality, although there is a delightful film called *Woman Of The World* (1923) which has something going for it – if only because it seemed to parallel Pola Negri's real-life situation. In it she plays a Polish Countess stranded in a Mid-west town. The very fact of her foreignness brings out all the inherent snobberies and prejudices of the local inhabitants. It was, for a Negri vehicle, of a lighter touch than usual and she carried it off extraordinarily well.

Her private life – immediately made public by newspapers and magazines aware that they were chronicling the doings of immortals – was as exotic as were her movies. She had a long-running love-affair with Rudolph Valentino after his divorce. His sudden death while she was in Los Angeles and he was in New York, prompted her to make a cross-country train trip which was accompanied by newspapermen who mercilessly mocked her extravagant displays of emotion. 'She swoons as often as ordinary people blow their noses,' wrote one. Her appearance at the funeral itself was similarly drenched with emotion and tears. But Mr. and Mrs. America, who might well have been enraptured by her European sensuality in her early days in the United States, were by now turned off by such a European display of grief. Letters appeared in the papers lamenting or making fun of such exhibitionism. Besides which, talkies were about to come in and the kind of movies in which she had appeared, already seemed outdated.

Described as 'a mistress of moods and a creature of exotic whims', she went back to Europe to pick up her career. She didn't

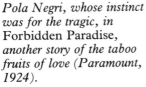

Pola Negri, whose instinct was for the tragic, in Forbidden Paradise, *another story of the taboo fruits of love (Paramount, 1924).*

A wistful Norma Talmadge – the girl next door raised to the power of classicism.

pick up too badly, either, appearing in some movies which were at least more presentable vehicles than some in which she had been ensconced in Hollywood. Her taste for interesting lovers, too, was unabated. She was not Jewish, as was so often supposed and, in fact, one of her great and good friends – to use the 'Time' magazine euphemism – was said to be Adolf Hitler. The tragedienne and the tragedy-maker. Now there's a piquant thought!

The Girl Next Door

There was still room though in the great big Hollywood heart for goddesses like that perpetual symbol of small-town America, the girl next door. Possibly the most famous of these was Norma Talmadge. There were, in fact, three Talmadge sisters, Constance, Natalie and Norma. All three went into the film business, driven there by a stage-mother of the most clichéd kind who was anxious to further her own ambitions via

those of her children. Constance was main-ly to be seen in sophisticated comedies, while Natalie – after an initial break-in – became better known as the wife of Buster Keaton, appearing in his *Our Hospitality* (1923). But if our kind of screen goddess is one who makes an imprint upon the hearts and minds of those who worship, then Norma is our girl!

She was for a long time the great special-ist in women's weepies, appearing first as the pathetic little milliner in the 1911 ver-sion of Dickens' *A Tale Of Two Cities*. It was a better thing she did then than she had done before, because her kind of quality-pathos was noted – and it sustained her reputation for ever after. The historian John Kobal has written that her *métier* was established in such a movie as *Panthea* (1917) in which she was 'a tragic and self-sacrificing heroine in beautiful clothes who sheds tears amid opulent surroundings and finds redemption just before the fade-out'.

It probably helped that she was married for a time to one of the most influential of all film producers, Joseph Schenck, who took over her career in 1916 and established what was to be known as the Norma Talmadge Film Corporation which distributed her movies first through First National and then through United Artists.

The coming of sound practically destroyed her career – 'Time' magazine described her as sounding like an elocution teacher – and, again, the vogue for her kind of high-gloss women's fiction was being shredded by the new reality of the late 1920s (although it was to re-emerge anew with Norma Shearer as one of its leading advocates).

Louise Brooks

I have called this section 'A Pantheon Of Primitives,' but there was nothing primitive – apart from the innate passion – in such goddesses as Louise Brooks who, after a period in Hollywood, went to Germany and made such films as *Pandora's Box* (1928) and *Diary Of A Lost Girl* (1929) for the great German director G.W. Pabst.

Nothing became Louise Brooks so much in life as her leaving Hollywood. As her memoirs reveal, she was a highly intelligent, as well as a most attractive, woman who realized the opportunities that Pabst offered – and took them, instead of the fruitless options of Hollywood. Her *Pandora's Box* is a transformation of Frank Wedekind's plays about Lulu, the amoral creature who drove men to suicide, women to lust after her body, and herself to a final meeting with the ultimate in orgiastic lovers, Jack The Ripper.

For a time the luminous vision of her sensuality, of which her mouth spoke nothing but her body said all, was one of the most pleasurable on the European film scene. Then, apart from some odd film pleasures, she was seen no more – only to be recalled later, when the writer Kenneth Tynan interviewed her in her old age.

Louise Brooks having to choose between lesbian countess and millionaire husband in Pandora's Box *(Nero Film, 1929). Her answer: she chose both.*

MOTION PICTURE

CLASSIC

JULY   25¢

Clara Bow

Senator Copeland On the Movies

and THE STORY OF INCEVILLE

The 'It' Girl makes it onto the fan-magazine cover: Clara Bow, the girl approved of by Elinor Glyn.

The 'It' Girl

Louise Brooks was worshipped by fans, even though they might account themselves to be intellectually above that description. But it was not often that the fan herself became the star – although that was the promise held out by Hollywood and nourished by the fan magazines themselves.

Clara Bow was different. She it was who was called the 'It' Girl by the romantic writer, Elinor Glyn, who was to the sexual mores of her time what Barbara Cartland is today, all purple eyes and purpler passion. She was responsible for the idea that making love on a tiger skin was somehow or other more erotic than conjoining on any other. 'How would you like to sin, with Elinor Glyn, On A Tiger Skin?' was a joke of the time.

'It' was simple sex appeal, tarted up as something else, something mysterious and snappy and just right for the preppy modern young thing of the time. So when a film was made of the Glyn novel, 'It', with Clara Bow starring, she became the 'It' girl. Clara Bow deserved all that was coming to her, in terms of fame and fortune. She seems by all accounts – and from the films one has seen of her – to have been a thoroughly pleasant and energetic person. She could so easily have been otherwise. Born in Brooklyn of a Coney Island waiter and a mentally unstable mother, she spent her childhood in poverty that by rights should have ground down her spirits – but, in fact, made her alert, quick-witted and spritely in her optimism that there was always hope – 'always something just around the corner'. For her, there was. When she was sixteen she won a fan magazine beauty contest and as a result got a small role in a film called *Beyond The Rainbow* (1922). It led to others, for she was a hard worker and eventually came *It* with her as Betty Lou the shopgirl who woos and then wows her millionaire boss.

What comes through in nearly all her movies is a flashy brilliance, an understanding – mute but more than adequately there – that sex is to be enjoyed and that, for flappers, she was very much one of them.

The coming of sound was not the only thing to help destroy her reputation, though it revealed her to be of a coarseness that silence had softened and made appealing.

What really damaged her was the discovery among the public that Miss Bow's private life was every bit as lurid as had been hinted at in her movies. There were alienated wives to be paid off in money and gambling debts to be paid off in court appearances and the ultimate besmirching when she sued her secretary, Daisy, for embezzlement and was in turn accused of drugs and drink and sex and worse . . . . The public lapped it up like poisoned milk, for the fall of goddesses is like no other because it is mighty and shows how far a fall there can be . . . .

Clara Bow stayed on into the sound-era but her films became fewer and fewer. She was still cast as the 'It' girl who was very much her own woman – the critic David Robinson has described it as being a combination of sex-kitten and militant virgin – but the parade had gone by, as it had for so many goddesses of the silent screen. The coming of sound meant the end for so many of them. The world would not see their like again. But there would be others of a different kind.

Woman as happy predator: Clara Bow with the about-to-be-ensnared Antonio Moreno in It *(Paramount, 1927). The name of the game was getting a man.*

Sound Stuff

In moving away from the time when silence was golden into that temporal location when sound was the stuff that box-office dreams were made of, almost inevitably one ought – by all the laws of film authorship – to begin with Greta Garbo, who was to use sound to express her emotions almost Delphically, as much in the omission as in the commission. But, authors, like the pre-feminist view of women, are allowed to be contrary, so I begin this section with a dissertation on one who pushed soundtrack decibels almost to their ultimate; whose shrill notes of fear and desperation refrigerated even the most masculine and stalwart of backbones. I refer, of course, to Fay Wray.

If a woman film-star becomes a goddess because of the company she keeps, then Fay Wray can be accounted a goddess purely by association, by becoming the sex-object of the affections of *King Kong* (1933), the vast special-effects ape, whose image of inherent *l'amour fou* lay across that portion of cinema history and whose gentle brutishness is still evoked in cinema today. King Kong became a folk-hero of the most monstrous and yet noble kind – a Caliban made god-like. He took Miss Wray along with him. For ever after she was to be associated as his alone, the love of his tormented, prehistoric life. 'Only connect', E.M. Forster has written. But how – audiences wondered, consciously and subconsciously – could Kong have ever made the sexual connection with Miss Wray. That he didn't was part of his inherently courteous nature. King Kong was not only monarch of all he surveyed in the way of our id and psyche, but he was a gentleman.

So if a screaming Fay Wray had not existed it might have been necessary to invent her – if only to prove that the soundtrack was resilient enough to withstand her slashing vocalizings. But Fay Wray had existed before Kong and had already achieved a certain reputation in films. Again, she seems to have been pushed hard by a persuasive stage-mother.

Born in Alberta, Canada, she moved to Los Angeles with her parents and attended Hollywood High School. She did the usual

Fay Wray gets the big-poster treatment for Legion Of The Condemned *(1928) in which she starred with Gary Cooper – before his 'yup-nope' days.*

extra work, but was turned down by Century Studios when taken there by her mother. The break came when Erich von Stroheim chose her for the female lead in *The Wedding March* (1926). Her description of this encounter and her realization that she had the role has a naivety which makes it touching and emotional; it was a quality she was to make manifest in all her parts. Perhaps that quality appealed to Kong . . . . The name of the girl Fay wanted to play was called Mitzi.

'Von Stroheim sat behind his desk and in a corner sat his secretary, Mrs. Westland. Von Stroheim said nothing, but just stared at Fay with a basilisk glare. Then: ' "Who does she look like to you?" "Mitzi," said Mrs. Westland. That was all. Then he rose and approached me. He put his hand over mine: "Goodbye, Mitzi". 'I broke into tears. I couldn't help it. That part was right for me. I knew I would get it when I read it. But when von Stroheim said "Goodbye Mitzi" it was just too much. Mrs. Schley (from casting) cried, Mrs. Westland cried and there were tears in von Stroheim's eyes. They left me there, and I sat weeping in the dark.'

A cruelly sharp account of sexual manners and mores, *The Wedding March*

went – as was von Stroheim's wont – way over budget to well over $1,250,000. His arguments with the studio bosses went onwards and upwards into stratospheric heights that only a Fay Wray scream could have reached. Eventually, it was released, though there was much trouble about the print that von Stroheim allowed out of his hands – the front office executives had demanded so many cuts. So did many small-town cinemas in America, for whom the subtlest form of humour was a pratfall on a banana skin. For them, von Stroheim was indeed – what, as an actor, he played up to – 'The Man You Love To Hate'.

Said one exhibitor: 'It's a fourteen-reel, messed-up picture. We had it booked for three nights, but we didn't have the nerve to offer to show it the second night. In London or in some foreign country, in a big city where there are all classes of nationalities, it might be understood and called a big picture.' It was called a big picture – by big-city critics, some of whom counted it as one of the best movies ever made. What came out of all the furore, though, was that Fay Wray was a star – 'Hip-Hip-Hoo-Wray!' as one newspaper headline put it so elegantly. In 1928 she appeared in three more movies: *Street Of Sin*, *The First Kiss* and *Legion Of*

'I don't think you ought to look dear.' Joel McCrea protects Fay Wray while a sinister Leslie Banks looks on in Hounds Of Zaroff (*1932*).

The Condemned, with Gary Cooper as her leading man in two of those films. Then, in 1929, she appeared in one of the earliest versions of *The Four Feathers* for the film-makers Merian C. Cooper and Ernest B. Schoedsack, who were to make *King Kong*, but there were other films in between which projected an image of vulnerable innocence not without a certain inner tensile strength.

In 1932 she made her first horror film, *Doctor X* with Lionel Atwill killing under a full moon. It was directed by Michael Curtiz, a Hungarian who sublimated his fascination with an Expressionist style to accommodate Hollywood methods and was to become one of the greatest and most productive of all commercial directors. Then followed *The Most Dangerous Game*, known in Britain as *The Hounds Of Zaroff*, about a big-game hunter Count Zaroff (Leslie Banks) hunting down humans as the ultimate sport – Joel McCrea and Fay Wray were his prey.

After that there were a couple more horror films, such as *Vampire Bat* (1933) – the title tells all – and *The Mystery Of The Wax Museum* (1933). I quote from 'American Silent Film' by the film historian William K. Everson: 'Fay Wray gets into the film quite late . . . and really has nothing to do other than provide a luscious victim for Lionel Atwill in the closing reels. Incidentally, Miss Wray – first seen doing her exercises in sweater and brief shorts – looks most fetching in Technicolor. She also doubles for the wax figure of Marie Antoinette in the opening reel – none too convincingly.' The director was again Michael Curtiz and Everson continues: 'Why Curtiz didn't shoot a few seconds and freeze-frame it, I don't know – the shot goes on endlessly and Miss Wray can be seen all too clearly breathing, twitching, moving her eyes, and even allowing some muscle movement of her right shoulder.' One must never, of course, allow muscle movement of the right shoulder, not even the left

shoulder . . . but such criticisms were to be forgotten when the mighty Kong was unleashed upon a waiting world.

In later years Fay Wray recalled the build-up towards being offered the rôle: 'I knew two very fine producers – Merian C. Cooper and his partner Ernest B. Schoedsack – and I admired the work that they had done. Mr. Cooper said to me that he'd had an idea for a film in mind. The only thing he'd tell me was that it was going to have "the tallest leading man in Hollywood" .... Well, naturally, I thought of Clark Gable hopefully, and when the script came I was absolutely appalled. I thought it was a practical joke. I really didn't have much appetite for doing it, except that I did admire these two people and I realized that it did at least have scope and a good imagination. It had dimension above anything else that had been tried in films.'

Its special effects are still talked about today and Bruce Cabot, Fay's leading man in *King Kong*, told me: 'That was the worst

part of it. You were playing to a character – a huge, huge character – who wasn't there. You began to get an inferiority complex about it all. Were the special effects more important than you were? Well, of course they were, but you didn't want your ego to get a downer by admitting it to yourself. I remember I went off and got terribly drunk for a couple of days, just to show that my absence could affect the film. But when I got back I found that they'd just shot around me. It was the special effects – and Fay Wray. She screamed and screamed, poor kid, until her throat was sore and she sounded so hoarse. But she does put something into the film; her personality *does* stand up to mighty Kong.'

It took nearly a year and a half just to fulfil to special effects, the assembly of Kong's personality, and it cost nearly a million dollars. A scene in which Kong fumbles off Fay Wray's blouse was deleted at the time, but restored in late prints. Beauty and the beast were thus reunited in

Lionel Atwill waxing eloquent over Marie Antoinette in The Mystery Of The Wax Museum *(Warner, 1933). Ms. Antoinette was Fay Wray.*

the inherent sexuality that was always implied. Miss Wray screamed throughout. She explained later: 'I just imagined I was miles from help and you'd scream too if you just imagined that situation with that monster up there. And when the picture was finished, they took me into the sound room, and then I screamed some more for about five minutes – just steady screaming, and they'd edit that and add it in.'

Fay Wray is probably the most passive of all our cinematic goddesses. As Ivan Butler wrote in 'Horror In The Cinema': 'Kong himself radiates charm, and easily wins our sympathy from his captors who deserve worse than they get. Fay Wray, the perfect heroine in such circumstances, would have softened tougher hearts than the old ape's, and their scenes together, as she lies cradled in his gentle palm, make us wish that he could have had a better chance of winning

her over to a greater appreciation of his own warm regard for her.'

The science fiction writer Ray Bradbury said in 'Scream Queens': 'You can't invent soul, as we all know. It simply happens. Even Mr. Cooper and Mr. Schoedsack, after they birthed Kong from their hot-wired ganglions and the brighter bumps on their heads, could not conceive or deliver forth anything as grand, as beautiful, as touching or as perfect as this God of the Apes.'

Or this Fay Wray whom the God of the Apes thought of as goddess. Miss Wray went on to do many more films, but with *King Kong* she reached a kind of height from which to look down at the rest of us poor mortals. So we'll leave her there, high at the top of the Empire State Building – and even higher in the esteem of Kong himself.

Greater love hath no Kong than that he lay down the life of a pterodactyl for his beloved. A scene from King Kong *(RKO, 1933).*

Garbo

It is doubtful if Greta Garbo ever uttered any kind of scream on cinema-soundtrack, though doubtless she was screaming inside when she saw – in the early days of her contract – just what MGM planned to do with her and her career; how they planned to make her into their kind of star, via podgy pin-ups and a scaffolding of gossip which would explain her 'foreignness' to the vast American public. It may have been because of that early horrendous experience that Greta Garbo achieved the reputation of wanting to be alone. Even David Niven – the most sociable of men – after spending time with her on a small boat, remarked how little he still knew her.

Nevertheless, Greta Garbo became, in the Thirties, one of the most remarkable goddesses to illumine the worship of the public. Numerous books have been written about why that should have been so. Was it her androgynous quality that seemed to beckon to both male and female alike? Was it that quality of stillness which people reckoned in the Turbulent Thirties and found peace there? Was it the fact – the most possible and plausible of all – that she was just a splendid actress for the screen who realized that underplaying was exactly what the camera wanted from her?

She never screamed so far as I know, but on screen her guttural mutter was as sexual an invitation as any 'Come up and see me some time' from an actress as blatant as Mae West. And when she laughed in *Ninotchka* – 'Garbo Laughs!' boasted the publicity headlines – it was a full-blown guffaw of life-enjoying richness; not a barmaid cackle, nothing as common as that – but vastly enhancing, nevertheless.

The mighty Kong was the star, but King Kong did give Fay Wray some good billing – and a chance to win a reputation as a screamer. 'That's all I seemed to do at times', she said.

Our goddess was born and called Greta Louisa Gustafsson in 1905 in Stockholm, Sweden, the daughter of a peasant labourer. She grew up in grinding poverty – and her father died when she was 13. The actress Mai Zetterling once told me: 'I'm a survivor. All Swedish girls are survivors: Ingrid Bergman, Garbo, me . . . we usually come from the same backgrounds: there's something in our stock that ensures that we'll get through whatever the adversity.'

For Greta there was a good deal of adversity. She found work in a men's barber's shop and, later, got a job as a salesgirl in a department store. She participated in a series of short publicity films for the store and, because of this and her realization that acting was for her, she won a scholarship to the training school of the Royal Dramatic Theatre. There she came under the influence of the man who was to shadow the early part of her career – for the better. This was Mauritz Stiller, a film director who was looking for a young actress to play a small-ish rôle in his forthcoming movie, *The Story Of Gösta Berling*. He was introduced to the girl who was to become Garbo and became her mentor and coach and, let it be said, father-figure – a Dad-shaped hole that had not yet been filled and which was not satisfyingly crammed by Stiller's presence.

Film historian Ephraim Katz quotes in *The International Film Encyclopedia* that, years later, Stiller revealed: 'I immediately noticed how easily one could dominate her by looking straight into her eyes'. Svengali and Trilby? The comparison was noted, but it is ironic that although Stiller started out as the teacher, it was in fact Garbo's inherent talent that gave him, for a time, a meal-ticket to Hollywood. For, in 1924 the MGM production chief Louis B. Mayer visited Europe on a talent-scouting expedition and was talked into taking on the rather clumsy-looking, undoubtedly big-boned girl – along with Stiller. She had, by that time, more experience in German movies, but MGM in Hollywood didn't know what to do with her, calling her such things as 'The Swedish Sphinx'. 'Here is a woman from Sweden who is like no other star you have seen. She is as inscrutable as any vamp from Egypt and yet she has a sensuousness which speaks to all men and all people.' (Even then her appeal to women was noted.) 'She is all woman. ALL WOMAN.'

There were arguments between studio executives and Stiller himself and Garbo was put into a film called *The Torrent* (1925). It was, to put it mildly, a revelation. Not so much because it was such a remarkable movie, but because of Garbo's quality which was exposed.

Rows still persisted with Stiller and he was replaced by director Fred Niblo on her next film, which was called *The Temptress* (1927). In that same year, Stiller returned to Sweden, a man broken by Hollywood and – seemingly – by the fact that his protégée, Garbo, had not returned with him. She had stayed to become a star. The daughter had renounced the 'father'. It is said that ever after she felt guilt for that 'betrayal' and that the famous scene in *Queen Christina* when she goes around the bedroom – after her lover has left – touching what they have touched, was a memory of what she and Mauritz Stiller had gone through together, because, he died only a few months later in Sweden, perhaps believing that Galatea had devoured Pygmalion . . . .

Whatever happened, Garbo did not talk about it. She had developed her own mystique, her own myth that she was not to be spoken to, that she was of herself alone. In an age of cinematic hype this was, of course, the ultimate hype. The great picture-going public might deign to love its heroes and heroines as and when it chose. It could not understand that a star need not feel the urge to love in return. So, like a puppy-dog that feels rejected, audiences rolled over – in a manner of speaking – and made her not just a star but a goddess. The box-office registers rang like a carillon of bells!

Her private affairs remained forever private, though inevitably, news and gossip leaked out. Certainly the affair with actor John Gilbert could not be disguised. It was so obvious that the embraces filmed in their co-starring *Flesh And The Devil* (1926) – the year that Mauritz Stiller returned to Sweden – were for real. And in *Queen Christina* (1933) it was again certain that those kisses meant more than just filmic make-believe.

Even when Gilbert's fortunes had declined into drink, because of the way the newly-arrived sound treated his voice – though some said that the vindictive Louis B. Mayer had fixed this – Garbo was loyal

to him, asking for him to appear on as many movies as she dare without jeopardizing her own career which was soaring off into the stratosphere.

There was talk of an impending marriage to the director Rouben Mamoulian – it never materialized – and of affairs with the conductor Leopold Stokowski. The nutrition expert Gaylord Hauser boasted in a newspaper article about his love affair with her; and the photographer Cecil Beaton was similarly skittish about what he said might have developed into a deep romance – a question, here, of pitching camp a little too blatantly, one would have thought.

She chose her movies not wisely but too well, although some of them, such as *Anna Karenina* (1935), completely fulfil the high romantic idealism that is therein contained. The critic Alexander Walker has written marvellously about Garbo but even for him,

her intangibility is something that eludes a pinning-down definition. The historian David Thomson, though, has a point when he writes in *A Biographical Dictionary of the Cinema*: 'Her essence is a matter of myth and the conjunction of natural performance with legendary and supernatural personality. She speaks and appears on behalf of the millions of plain people who require a lofty She who must be obeyed, but who can see in her the elevated traces of their own inadequacy and diffidence. The goddess must be indifferent to her worshippers, not quite able to concentrate on them. That feeling of distraction draws them to her so much more securely and confirms their secret belief that she too has worries, anxieties, moments of defeat.'

Garbo's shrewdness – the shrewdness of her native Sweden – was apparent in the way she had herself photographed. While she was never as understanding of

Above: Garbo and John Gilbert in Flesh And The Devil *(MGM, 1926). Their on-screen love went off-screen, too.*

Opposite: Garbo in The Torrent *(MGM, 1925).*

61

Opposite: Already the air of sexual self-sacrifice is apparent on Garbo's face in Anna Karenina *(MGM, 1935).*

photographic technique as Marlene Dietrich – who had, after all, been coached by Josef von Sternberg – she knew the value of back-lighting and always asked for cameraman William Daniels who worked on twelve of her fourteen sound movies. He has written: 'She was always taken in close-ups or long shots, hardly ever intermediate or full figure. The latter did not come out well.' This may well have been because Garbo was somewhat ungainly. But despite that, careful photographic grooming ensured that she appeared with the grace of a goddess on screen.

There is always, of course, a quality in us that wants to bring a goddess down to our plane of mundane reality. So it was with Garbo: to reveal her as a plastic puppet waiting to be moulded by the men around her. To an extent that is true, but her instinct for success, her ability to control that

success when it came, seems to me to be truly her own work.

Clarence Brown, the director, who worked with Garbo six times once repeated to me what he had said to others: 'Garbo had something behind the eyes that you couldn't see until you photographed it in close-up. You could see thought. If she had to look at one person with jealousy and another with love, she didn't have to change her expression. You could see it in her eyes as she looked from one to another.' Such qualities, of course, may just as easily be in the eye of the beholder – projecting into the image his or her own thoughts about the events depicted. But even the fact that Garbo was a vessel-image for such projections proves just what a star she was.

Rouben Mamoulian, who directed her in *Queen Christina*, says about her famous final shot when she stares into space as the

Below: Garbo tastes forbidden fruit with John Gilbert in Queen Christina *(MGM, 1933).*

MGM's LAUGH HIT IS HERE!

NINOTCHKA

(Don't pronounce it...
SEE IT!)

STARRING

Greta GARBO

The Picture that kids the Commissars!

WITH
MELVYN DOUGLAS · INA CLAIRE

AN ERNST LUBITSCH PRODUCTION

SCREEN PLAY BY CHARLES BRACKETT, BILLY WILDER AND WALTER REISCH · BASED ON THE ORIGINAL STORY BY MELCHIOR LENGYEL

DIRECTED BY ERNST LUBITSCH

A METRO-GOLDWYN-MAYER MASTERPIECE REPRINT

Above: Well, we all knew Garbo could laugh, didn't we? It was Lubitsch who gave her the opportunity.

Opposite: Garbo as the public had grown to know her – stern, severe but very easy to worship.

ship bearing her away plunges through the ocean, that he told her to think of nothing. Others may think that the comment is rather down-putting and derogatory. But looking at the film again you realize that, in that look her nothings seem far more important and mystical than the somethings of many other stars.

In her films she usually played rôles that were doomed by the urging of love, but she was not always well served by her choices. Her last film, *Two-Faced Woman* (1941), does not do her credit. My favourite rôle of hers is that of the communist *Ninotchka* (1939), in which Lubitsch shows the sentiment at the heart of cynicism by telling the story of a stony-faced woman commissar of the people who is seduced by Paris and Melvyn Douglas. In that she laughs and copes with some of writer Billy Wilder's most outrageous double-entendres – as when she asks Douglas if he would like to see her wound . . . only she could get away

with that with dignity. And she had that, all right. The dignity of her fabulous femininity.

It is sad that, for Garbo's twenty-seventh and final film, she should have been involved in something as wrong for her as *Two-Faced Woman*, in which she played a ski-instructress in a tedious amorous entanglement with Melvyn Douglas. The 'New York Times' wrote: 'this is clearly one of the less propitious assignments of her career. Though she is her cool and immaculate self . . . she is as gauche and stilted as the script. This is 1941/42 and Theda Bara's golden age is gone!'

Noting that 'Time' magazine also said that the film was 'not unlike seeing Sarah Bernhardt swatted with a bladder . . . as shocking as seeing your mother drunk', it is intriguing to note that, in fact, the golden age of Theda Bara did live on . . . in one who at one time had been touted as a rival to Garbo: Marlene Dietrich.

Dietrich

Dietrich was the vamp transformed into high art, into bewilderment for the male psyche; a woman who took love – in the genteel fashion of Hollywood cinema – and could make it seem very like lust in the way she mocked the glands that could make fools of herself and whichever leading man was cast as her lover. Again, there was a certain androgynous quality about her, mostly seen in her private life when she would attend premières and parties clad in a man's dress-suit – and looking ultra-female, perhaps because of that contrast in garb. Some writer once quoted about Marlene Dietrich what was said about Trilby in the novel of that name by George du Maurier: 'She was one of those rarely gifted beings who cannot look or speak or even stir without waking up (and satisfying) some vague longing that lies dormant in the hearts of most of us.'

She was born in 1901 in a middle-class district of West Berlin as Maria Magdalene Dietrich, the daughter of a Prussian officer. She became obsessed by the theatre when she was a teenager and then drifted into German movies.

She was a rising star in the German film firmament and the meeting with director Josef von Sternberg was to spin her higher still up the arc of celebrity. It was, without doubt, Sternberg who created the vampish image that is all we know of early Dietrich.

Marlene Dietrich, seen through Josef von Sternberg's eyes as Prince Slut in The Blue Angel *(UFA, 1930).*

He takes credit for that, with an egotistical intensity which perhaps shows a certain insecurity. By the time they parted from each other, he was coldly calling her 'Frau' and dismissing her as a 'Hausfrau'. She was more than that . . . and he knew it. But to him must go that initial credit. For he wanted her for the vamp-rôle of Lola-Lola in his *The Blue Angel* (1930) – the woman who corrupts the harsh, ageing schoolmaster of Emil Jannings and brings him to a gutter-level he had never even dreamed of.

Said von Sternberg in *Fun In A Chinese Laundry*: 'I then put her into the crucible of my conception, blended her image to correspond with mine, and, pouring lights on her until the alchemy was complete, proceeded with the test. She came to life and responded to my instructions with an ease that I had never before encountered. She seemed pleased at the trouble I took with her, but she never saw the test I made, nor ever asked to see it. Her remarkable

vitality had been channelled.'

.The success of *The Blue Angel* took Dietrich to Hollywood with von Sternberg, who became known – because of his effect on Dietrich – as 'Svengali Joe'. It is worth noting that it was not the gullible American public alone that fell for her allure. Other professionals fell before her, including John Barrymore who said: 'She handles her body like Stradivarius used to handle his violins. And no matter what kind of finish it happens to be wearing at the time, it's still a masterpiece!'

There followed for Marlene Dietrich a series of films for von Sternberg which, inevitably – since that is how he had first seen her – cast her in the rôle not only as *femme fatale* but of *femme fatalistic*, life-weary because of what life and love has done to her. *Morocco* (1930), for instance, had her as Amy Jolly, a cabaret entertainer – which seems to be a euphemism for a groupie for the Foreign Legion – who is

Right: Marlene – as seen by von Sternberg again – in The Scarlet Empress, *his stylized view of Russia's Catherine the Great (Paramount, 1934).*

Below: A less overwrought Marlene with Gary Cooper in Desire *(Paramount, 1936).*

smitten by Legionnaire Tom Brown (Gary Cooper). Tom Brown's amorous fooldays are not yet over, but for him Amy will make the sacrifice. As the synopsis put it: 'She was the cool, calculating woman whose past had brought her nothing but misery. Determined to change all that, she chases her man first with subtle charms then openly defying all standards and customs. They matter not to her. The wealthy artist offers marriage, wealth and security which indeed tempt her – as before. But she finally listens to herself and goes after the cynical legionnaire who has turned away from her.' To that extent, she becomes a camp follower, pursuing her man out into the wind-ravaged desert (but first removing her shoes which have heels at least three inches high!).

There is, within the titles themselves, a whole area of cinematic emotion expressed by the films she made for von Sternberg: *Dishonoured* (1931), *Shanghai Express* (1932), *Blonde Venus* (1932), *The Scarlet Empress* (1934), *The Devil Is A Woman* (1935) . . . the art of the matter was the cynical heart of the matter. Von Sternberg saw her as the all-consuming woman, powerful in her mystery and, even when revealed, still mysterious in that revelation.

There was, to be true, little of the humour that other directors were to reveal within the Dietrich fable. She made films for other great directors, such as Frank Borzage (*Desire* – 1935), and slowly that quality was displayed and became part of the Marlene Dietrich legend. About *Desire*, for instance, 'The New York Times' noted that Ernst Lubitsch (who produced it): ' . . . has freed Marlene Dietrich from Josef von Sternberg's artistic bondage and has brought her vibrantly to life in *Desire* . . . . Permitted to walk, breathe, smile and shrug as a human being instead of a canvas for the Louvre Miss Dietrich recaptures . . .

The Devil Is A Woman
(*Paramount, 1935*). *A
title to sum up a whole
view of womankind.
Directed by Josef von
Sternberg, of course.*

some of the freshness and gaiety of spirit that was hers in *The Blue Angel* and other of her early successes.'

The magazine 'Vanity Fair' had also had its doubts about whether von Sternberg was continuing to be good for Dietrich. After *The Scarlet Empress* its critic wrote: 'Sternberg traded his open style for fancy play, chiefly upon the legs in silk and buttocks in lace, of Dietrich, of whom he had made a paramount slut. By his own token, Sternberg is a man of meditation as well as a man of action: but instead of contemplating the navel of Buddha, his umbilical perseverance is fixed on the navel of Venus.' It is also to be noted that Mrs. von Sternberg sued for divorce and, among her reasons for naming Dietrich was that she had been responsible for 'alienating the affections of my husband'.

Certainly, Dietrich's ambisexual persona did her no harm at the box-office, despite a scene in *Morocco* in which – as the club entertainer – she kisses a woman member of her audience. She herself was happily married for a time and had a family. What she

got from von Sternberg was an understanding of the quality of how to light herself properly. She sometimes put up a little rear-view mirror so that she could see herself how the camera saw her. It was an aptitude for the exploitation of herself, which provoked sour comments from Alfred Hitchcock when he directed her in *Stage Fright* (1950), but which she never forgot – and was always to use to her advantage.

There was a much-quoted occasion when she was aware that the cameraman of her new film was not lighting her with the requisite amount of attention, not lavishing upon her the illumination that helped her to preserve her image of goddess. She argued with the man several times and then stood looking down at the floor, moaning softly and piteously: 'Where are you Joe?' Marlene Dietrich knew who had helped create her; even though she was now a big girl and could stand on the illusion of her own personality as though it were real, firm ground, she was under no illusions herself as to whom she owed the creation.

Blonde Bombshells

Goddesses stand in their niches above the rest of frail humanity, but the sound-films of the 1930s showed that they could also descend and walk among us – and still keep the integrity of their own deity. Two platinum blondes correspond to that definition, and their deification was considerably enhanced by soundtrack which recorded their slangy wisecracks and their repartee which zinged back at whoever had bounced it at them in the first place. I refer to Jean Harlow and Mae West – the first the shopgirl/barmaid transformed by Hollywood magic, and her own innate ability, into a shining goddess-spectacle; the other an ample grotesque whose own *chutzpah* conned and wooed millions into believing that she stood for something permissively modern and sexual (when, in fact, the very corsetry of her attire was of that libidinous nature that belonged to an earlier century – like a Victorian wet dream).

Jean Harlow was a good-time girl who, in the last resort, would help you out of the

Opposite: Marlene Dietrich as the epitome of the sophisticated lady. Svelte, cool and radiating sexual self-confidence.

Left: The shape of cinematic sex to come with Jean Harlow – frank, provocative and still desirable.

dilemma into which, doubtless, she had helped plunge you. Her hair betokened flash, as did her Clara Bow-like lips. But in so many of her films there was the implication that underneath she was 'all right'. It was the men who – in Mae West's definition – might well have 'done her wrong'.

After her film *Bombshell* (1933), the 'New York Herald Tribune' wrote of her: '. . . as a bewildered, hectically-living film star, who combines a love of exhibitionism with a certain wistful desire for home and babies – a part which might easily have been transformed into an orgy of embarrassing sentimentality – Miss Harlow reveals again that gift for an amalgamation of sophisticated sex comedy with curious honest innocence which is the secret of her individuality. There can be no doubt now that she is a distinguished performer. *Bombshell* is important as another step in Miss Harlow's career.' In truth, and paradoxically, the role in *Bombshell* was close enough to home to the real Jean Harlow.

Jean Harlow emerged into the world that she was to treat with a certain cynical disdain as Harlean Carpenter in Kansas City, Missouri in 1911. In 1937, at the age of twenty-six, she was dead. Around her was built a Monroe-like legend, but you feel – with Harlow – that she was much more in control of what she was. It may have been a careless carnality, but she knew that it could get her what she wanted.

Life for her seemed like one of those quickfire, sure-thing scenarios which she made her own in the 1930s. At the age of sixteen she had eloped with a millionaire, but quickly divorced him – 'It's all that hot Southern blood', she later said – and worked as an extra in movies, including some early Laurel and Hardy films. The millionaire-eccentric Howard Hughes chose her to replace Greta Nissen in *Hell's Angels* (1930), that spectacular movie about flying – which was more famous in its own day than it could ever be now, so peculiarly dated is it. Interestingly enough, though, Harlow's brand of sly, candid suggestiveness – if that is not too paradoxical a description – even managed to upstage some of the aerial stunts. Her own high-flying was, meanwhile, being done off-set.

She worked with some fine directors, from William Wellman's *The Public Enemy* (1931) to Frank Capra's *Platinum Blonde* (1931), a livewire comedy about a newspaperman and an heiress which was at once sexy and comic. The 'New York Daily Mirror' licked its lips and said: 'Miss Harlow flaunts the famous Harlow figure . . . .' She did indeed. In 'A Biographical Dictionary of the Cinema' historian David Thomson comments on the way 'Capra randily photographed Harlow's body. One shot, tracking with Harlow, is an unashamed sexual homage, a desert island shot.'

Her rôle with Clark Gable in *Red Dust* (1932) portrayed her as the rough girl who gets her man – a rubber plantationer – because of her directness and honesty. It was an art she was to cultivate, perhaps

because it was so much a part of the way she was in real life. But real life was more painful, if as direct.

Of all the scandals among the goddesses that slashed into the morality-mentality of the picturegoing public in the 1930s, the death of Jean Harlow's husband was one of the most traumatic. Paul Bern was twenty-two years older than Harlow and known as MGM's 'Father Confessor' for his ability to soothe and calm some of the more temperamental of his stars who were in trouble. He was assistant to Irving Thalberg at MGM

Made for each other – Clark Gable and Jean Harlow in Red Dust, *in which she played the definitive man's woman (MGM, 1932).*

"It'll break grandpa's heart if you sell him!"

and he and Harlow were married on July 2, 1932. Two months later he was found in Harlow's all-white bedroom, nude, sprawled in front of a full-length mirror and reeking of Harlow's favourite perfume, Mitsouko. He had shot himself with the gun that lay by his side. There was a letter, addressed to Jean Harlow:

'Dearest Dear,
Unfortunately this is the only way to make good the frightful wrong I have done you, and to wipe out my abject humiliation. I love you.
    Paul

You understand that last night was only a comedy.'

Impotence? That was what the gossips muttered about. And it was all made even more compromising because Louis B. Mayer, head of the studio, who was brought to look at the body before the police, pocketed that note. Only later was he persuaded to hand it over.

A goddess is a survivor – and Harlow survived that and more. The sudden and rapid exposure of the sadness of her private life was also matched by the slow revelation of her real ability in cinematic life. In *Dinner At Eight* (1933), for instance, she plays a scheming wife about whom Marie Dressler is not at all mistaken. Does the older woman think that machinery will take over things human, asks someone. Dressler watches Harlow walk in front of her, her posterior moving like two ferrets in a sack. There are some things that will never be replaced, she says.

Harlow was, in many senses of the word, a superstar, fit to be cast opposite such tough-talking, full-fisted male stars as Clark Gable or Spencer Tracy. She was their kind of girl, a man's woman. And yet there was something – again, a quality to notice in other goddesses – innocent and vulnerable beneath the surface gloss. She was, as somebody said at the time, 'cuddleable'. For all her wise-cracking, a man

Once again, the teaming of Jean Harlow with Clark Gable – this time in Saratoga *(MGM, 1937).*

75

Complete with phallic swan, Mae West looks all seductive for Cary Grant in She Done Him Wrong *(Paramount, 1933).*

might want to pamper and protect her from all the slings and arrows of an outrageous fortune.

She died of cerebral edema at, as I said, an astonishingly early age, and her life resulted in an expose-all biography in 1964 and two movies, both made in that year. One starred Carroll Baker and the other, Carol Lynley. Neither was up to the glitzy, glittery image that Jean Harlow had made hers. She was the best star of her own short life.

'When I'm Bad I'm Better'

Life, for Mae West, was similarly a screenplay, though in her case very much of her *own* invention. She was a coarsened version of what Jean Harlow was to become. There was nothing cuddly or vulnerable about her blonde aura which was not so much platinum as aluminium or cast-iron. She was the Iron Lady of Libido. She was born in August, 1892, in Brooklyn (where else?), the daughter of a heavyweight boxer (who else?) and somehow or other became an entertainer when she was only five years old. She later moved into burlesque (what else?), where the men paid to see strippers and groaned their way through the comedians. She made her mark in a genre which was, by all accounts, one of the toughest, bawdiest, sweatiest and most satisfying disciplines of all branches of show business. She had the dubious distinction of introducing the 'shimmy' to the stage – a way of writhing the lower half of the body as in a dance. Hence the song-title: 'If you could shimmy like my sister Kate . . .' – or words to that strange effect. In later life she was to be surrounded by muscle-men, one of whom, Mickey Haggerty, became the husband of a sex-symbol of the 1950s, Jayne Mansfield – the blonde-imprint was obviously still upon him – and her open avowal of her enjoyment of men made her a scandal in her own lustime.

She had become used to rewriting her stage material and she wrote a play called 'Sex' which in 1927 was stopped by the law and she was imprisoned for ten days for so-called obscenity. Then she wrote a play called 'Drag' (1932) which was about homosexuals. It was inevitable that after all this controversy – as always, a marvellous image-booster – she would be offered a film contract. And she was. By Paramount.

Her stars over the films she made ranged from Cary Grant to W.C. Fields and, in 1935, she was accounted the highest-paid woman in the United States. An inflatable life-jacket was named after her – or rather her bosom pals – by the American Navy. Her movies ranged from *She Done Him Wrong* (1933) to *My Little Chickadee* (1940). She returned briefly to the screen in 1978 for a disastrous adaptation of Gore Vidal's *Myra Breckinridge*. But even that monstrous movie could not erase the power of personality which had made its mark upon the ways of sexual enlightenment over the first half of the century. It was not that she brought sex out into the open – I have mentioned the Victorian aspect earlier – it is just

Mae West, arms at the washer-woman ready in characteristic pose – looking like a Victorian beauty queen in Klondike Annie *(Paramount, 1936).*

that she referred to it as something hugely enjoyable. She was the earthiest goddess in this compilation.

How did she achieve this? She had some great one-liners of dialogue. 'When I'm good I'm very good, but when I'm bad I'm better.' Or: 'Is that a pistol in your pocket or are you pleased to see me?' (this last to a man). Or again: 'It's not the man in my life, but the life in my man'.

There is a weird connection between Orson Welles and Mae West, in that both of them incurred the wrath of the newspaper tycoon William Randolph Hearst. Welles, of course, suffered from newspaper attacks because his *Citizen Kane* was based on Hearst. Hearst believed that Mae West had attacked the acting of his mistress, Marion Davies. In 1936 a Hearst newspaper trumpeted Mae West as 'a monster of lubricity' and for her movie *Klondike Kate* denounced her as 'a menace to the Sacred Institution of the American Family'.

Mae West's was the bosom that launched a thousand quips and it was these, besides the blatant purveying of sex, to which Hearst objected: 'Between two evils, I always pick the one I never tried before.' Hearst ordered that all advertisements for her films were to be banned from his papers.

Mae West's great virtue – and goodness, in the way of honesty, had a great deal to do with it – was that she was at once sex-symbol and sex-parody. She was sex raised to the power of mockery. She was of the earth and earthy and she made a heavenly thing of that which was supposed to be beneath the contempt of the moralists. Her later movies were bowdlerized, as it were, by remote control by a Hays Office which was, supposedly, much influenced by Hearst's hate of her – and the films went into decline. But it was not that so much that deflated her image as the way events were moving . . . .

Mae West with her favourite comedian W.C. Fields in My Little Chickadee (Universal, 1940). *He just about survived.*

MAE WEST · W.C. FIELDS
in
My Little Chickadee

A *NEW* UNIVERSAL PICTURE

Immigrant Goddesses

One of the unique qualities about Mae West was that she was superbly and supremely from America itself – the all-American woman. But it is intriguing to note that Hollywood, as though to keep fresh blood pumping around its tired old arteries, was constantly replenishing itself with would-be goddesses from Europe.

Anna Sten, for instance, came to Hollywood by way of Germany from Russia and was announced as a great discovery for producer Sam Goldwyn. Certainly, she had a feral sexual attraction, but she was always in the second-league of cinema goddesses, although her *The Wedding Night* (1935), directed by King Vidor, had the kind of over-the-top emotion that sends an audience out reeling. She dies by falling down a sinuously winding flight of stairs in the climax. It was a trick to be repeated, but rarely to recapture that first fine careless capture of melodramatic surprise. It was a

very European dénouement and we must never forget that – in the 1930s – it may well have been accounted as extraordinarily sophisticated. Although Hollywood ruled the box-office, America was aware that the virtues of drama and emotion might well reside across the Atlantic. This accounts for the emphasis on British Raj films in the 1930s – on which a whole colony of British actors relied for a living – and films which paid due respects to European culture in the way that Sam Goldwyn did with such movies as *Wuthering Heights* (1939).

Certainly there were home-grown American blooms around at the time, but the major blossoms were European orchids. There was the fabulously-featured Hedy Lamarr who rode to Hollywood on a crest of notoriety caused by her nude appearance in a Czechoslovak film, *Ecstasy* (1933). The millionaire-husband she later married in America was said to have tried to buy up every print of her nakedness, but was

Another lovely foreign import – Anna Sten in The Wedding Night *(Samuel Goldwyn, 1935). King Vidor thought she had a great sexual attraction. He should know – he directed her.*

Right: The beauty of Hedy Lamarr – seized by Hollywood after her nudie, Extase (Ecstasy).

Above: Ruby Keeler, the all-singing, all-dancing girl in 42nd Street (Warner, 1933).

Gaslight that Ingrid Bergman picked up to such luminous effect.

It was not just Lamarr's fault or the fault of her agent or manager. It was the way the world was moving as the Thirties died and were about to give birth to the Forties. Goddesses were not what they used to be – or, at any rate, they were different. The days were numbered when all Ruby Keeler had to do was to walk on and give a dimpled smile for audiences to fall over in a Lamarr-like ecstasy.

Canadian-born Ruby Keeler was, perhaps, typical of a particular manifestation of the American Thirties when dance-director Busby Berkeley and the studios gave the world 'Dames To Beat The Depression'. She was not as talented as her oft-time co-star Joan Blondell, but she laid out what talent she had and made it seem as though it were a lot. She will always be remembered as the cutie from the Warner Brothers' musicals of those Deprived Thirties. Although her career as any kind of superstar was only sustained for that period, she was nevertheless a kind of goddess. Her attraction was that if she could get into that niche above the rest – well, so could anyone else!

She too, was a chorus girl – rumoured to have been involved with gangsters – before she married Al Jolson. She worked for the great stage impresario Flo Ziegfeld and then went into the film *42nd Street* (1933) and later *Gold Diggers Of 1933* (1933): her winsome naïvety compared neatly with the sly lewdness that Dick Powell inveigled into numbers which, for their time, were a risqué business.

For that time she was a box-office magnet, drawing audiences. Was it because of charm or, as I mentioned, that feeling that if she could do it so could any other girl next door? In his book, 'Hollywood: A State Of Dreaming', Professor Burt Rainer, in referring to the musicals of the time, says: 'They were, of course, dreams to be dreamed with the eyes wide open for all those to whom reality at that time – with dole-queues and rumours of war and war itself – was a nightmare. A figure as frail in talent as was Ruby Keeler could yet be seen as a vessel into which all an audience's yearning could be poured. They knew the vessel could not sink because they knew – in real life – that Ruby Keeler was a film-star whose own world floated on riches and success. And

denied that monopolistic urge. Her first film was *Algiers* (1938) and, for a time, she was the acme of every acned youth's fevered dreams. But, although she was a goddess for a time, it was in reality only a short time. She had not the sustaining power and she chose wrongly. It is reported that she rejected the roles in *Casablanca* and

this, despite the fact that she could scarcely speak lines with any dramatic intonation or inflection. She was a repository of hope. If, at times, it could be thought that she was sleep-walking through a rôle – as indeed it sometimes seemed that she was – nevertheless that added to her attraction as a film-star. For just before the Second World War there was a sense in which everyone was a somnambulist. The cliff lay just ahead.'

That was the way the world was turning, the light shifting from one kind of star to another. No precise date to be placed as to where or when this actually happened. But it was, one could say, around 1939, as war engulfed Europe and the harsher light cast by shellfire illumined a new breed of god and goddess after the chandelier-fancies of the earlier times. And 1939 was the year of *Gone With The Wind*.

Dick Powell spelling it out to Ruby Keeler in Busby Berkeley's Gold Diggers of 1933 *(Warner, 1933). Risqué? That was a risk they took.*

A Different Class of Virgin

The coincidental emergence of *Gone With The Wind* with the opening of the Second World War seems entirely appropriate. For, looked at in retrospect, *Gone With The Wind* can be seen as perhaps the last of those extravagant romances – in which context screen goddesses could be seen to the best advantage – which the actuality of the wind of war was to blow away as so much romantic gossamer. Yet there was never such a need of that kind of romance, of that kind of relationship between a man and a woman as that between Clark Gable's Rhett Butler and Vivien Leigh's Scarlett O'Hara – soap-opera frothed up ahead of its televisual time. Escapist, of course, but what a world to escape into! And, for a time – brief enough, admittedly – it made a screen goddess of the cat-kittenish Vivien Leigh.

Born in India, Vivien Leigh had already achieved a small reputation in Britain and married Laurence Olivier in a well-publicized marriage. MGM's Louis B. Mayer thought she was too 'prissy' as an actress, so what was to be a large role in *A Yank At Oxford* became, for her, virtually a supporting one. *Gone With The Wind*, though, was David O. Selznick's big movie and Vivien Leigh's agent was David's brother, Myron .... David O. had taken and bought the rights of Margaret Mitchell's novel, fully aware that he was buying up the rights of a book which, to America, was a kind of middle-brow holy writ. It was a book whose sub-Tolstoyan story of love and betrayal amid Civil War carnage had achieved a reputation far in excess of its artistic achievement. Every woman – actress or not – wanted to play the wayward, but still sympathetic, Scarlett and David O. Selznick shrewdly cashed in on the interest by holding auditions for an actress to play her throughout the length and breadth of the United States. It was a formidable rôle because, although goddesses may allow themselves to fall from sexual grace, they must at the same time appear inviolable – that is part of their attraction. Some part of the feminine core of the screen goddess must not have been touched. Scarlett was a different class of virgin.

There is an inherent virginity that shapes the ends of a goddess; within her there is a quality that has not been breached. Yet Scarlett was wide open as a character and about as mysterious as a mirror; that is, as open to the interpretation of all who looked into the character and saw themselves therein reflected. Selznick himself saw that and wrote about it in those innumerable memos which were the bane and inspiration of those who worked with and for him. Bette Davis, Tallulah Bankhead and many others were among the women stars who gladly auditioned for the rôle, realizing that here was a plum part against which would be set their future careers. Still, Selznick could not make up his mind and had actually started filming . . .

The yarn is that while he was shooting the night scenes of the burning of Atlanta brother Myron came up to him with Vivien Leigh and said: 'David, this is your Scarlett' . . . or words to that apocryphal effect. For there are those who suggest that the whole thing had been cut and dried and Vivien Leigh contract-trussed before the whole charade had started. However . . . Vivien Leigh won an Oscar for her portrayal and other ceremonial bounties were heaped upon her, despite the antagonism of those who felt that the part of their so-American Scarlett should have gone to a native-born girl and not to some 'goddamned Britisher'. So, for a time, Vivien Leigh reigned as a goddess; her fashions were

Above: The embrace that said it all for a whole generation . . . and beyond. Clark Gable and Vivien Leigh getting it together in Gone With The Wind *(MGM/David O. Selznick, 1939).*

Left: Dinner is served for the two of them in the same film. But who could eat at a time like this?

emulated, as those of goddesses are, and her every saying was reported and recorded as though from some ancient oracle.

But more is required for the sustaining of a godhead. To an extent, Vivien Leigh was too good an actress, too intelligent a woman, to keep the whole thing going. It is by no means disrespectful to suggest that there has to be a limited purpose behind those who would achieve, and have achieved, the goddess-status. They have to believe in themselves utterly – in order that *others* may believe in them utterly. Having been trained for the stage, Vivien Leigh realized that her screen rôles and the role of Scarlett O'Hara were not the be-all and end-all of a life that had to be lived. By rights goddesses should squint, because they cannot see beyond the lovely nose on their face. Vivien Leigh was too far-sighted for that. In her private life, as Laurence Olivier has recorded, she was exhaustingly emotional, but she kept it for her private life. As the writer David Thomson wrote about her films: 'She lacked extravagance.'

Ingrid Bergman

The word 'extravagance' might seem not to apply to Ingrid Bergman, yet there is in all her screen portrayals a sense of arousal beneath the gentility, of passion beneath the demure exterior which contrasts well with the soft-eyed look. Another Swede – she was born in Stockholm – she came to prominence during the war, although she had achieved some success in films just before. Her quality was that withdrawn virginity which could flood open into unabashed passion. Of all our goddesses, she was one of the most romantic. An orphan – yet another who was, perhaps, searching for a father figure – she was brought up by relatives and, after a spell on the Swedish stage, came to Hollywood to star in the 1939 Hollywood version of *Intermezzo* with Leslie Howard. The public – American audiences especially – took to her persona with enthusiasm. She looked, as she later declared, 'milk-fed'. Her beauty seemed enormously natural; her make-up, if there was any, was of the very least.

In 1943 she appeared with Humphrey Bogart in *Casablanca* and the legend of that film and her own and all the others appearing were given a new boost, a new impetus into the annals of cinema. *Casablanca* is, to see it yet again, a fairly ramshackle affair with – as was admitted – a narrative-line which seems to have been made up as it went along. As seems to have been the case. But it is one of those movies that touches some folkloric nerve. It appeals over and

84

Ingrid Bergman – with tresses shorn – Katrina Paxinou and Gary Cooper in a somewhat sanitized version of Hemingway's For Whom The Bell Tolls *(Paramount, 1943).*

over again, to generations who have never seen it and who come upon it afresh and with delight. Not the least of its pleasures is that of Ingrid Bergman.

She was the girl-guerrilla in *For Whom The Bell Tolls* (1943) and the persecuted wife in *Gaslight* (1944). She was the psychiatrist loving the suspected murderer of Gregory Peck in *Spellbound* and she was the nun at odds with Bing Crosby in *The Bells Of St Mary's* (1945). She was America's darling because she seemed so unforced and unspoiled. She herself has said that this continued veneration in which she was held became more than a little wearing.

Goddesses are women, with all a woman's pain, problems and passions. How rarely can worshippers forgive if they realize that the object of worship is as they are – given to error. Ingrid Bergman had seen the film *Rome, Open City* by the Italian director Roberto Rossellini, a landmark in its wartime violence. Some of it was shot while the Germans were actually leaving Rome. That, and other movies, made cineastes realize that Rossellini was one whose potential was for greatness. Ingrid Bergman realized that as well. She wrote a fan-letter to Rossellini, as simple and as naïve as any teenage-girl's – offering her services for whatever film he might deem her fit for.

The result was that, in 1949, she left her dentist-husband, Dr. Peter Lindstrom, whom she had married in 1937, and went to live with Rossellini whom she married in 1950. American women were in an uproar! She was denounced by all those leagues who proliferate puritanically across America; the milk-fed image had soured with the revelation of the woman's infidelity. Not since Charlie Chaplin had been 'exposed' as a seducer of young girls had there been such a furore. Ingrid Bergman had, it seems, not just been unfaithful to her husband – but to the whole population of America.

Of course, it blew over . . . in time. But the love-affair between America and Ingrid Bergman could never be the same again. The goddess had proved to be standing on a very rickety pedestal. But there was always *Casablanca* to remember her by, and the song 'As Time Goes By' became synonymous with Bergman herself – the realization that time, and things physical, decay, but that love itself can continue forever, never ruinous, always enhancing. Never can a goddess have had such a theme-song.

Bergman reached her success-peaks during the Second World War and this was the time when heroines had to be diverting as well as desirable. They were, after all, to be used as implicit propaganda for troops facing conditions of hardship which were not to be imagined within Hollywood's philosophy. The musicals from such studios as Twentieth Century-Fox and MGM were the fabulous barges wherein lolled those women who were to excite the imagination – or at least irritate it, because once the serviceman became too desirous he might want to lay down his arms and take up more alluring ones.

A Pin-Up Goddess

Betty Grable was one of the most leggily illustrious of those stars whose context seems to have been solely the musical. Despite being contrivedly 'menaced' by her studio who brought in Alice Faye as a supposed replacement if ever Grable didn't sign on the dotted line of command, she nevertheless managed to project enough no-nonsense sexiness to pitch her up there among the goddesses, even if on a lower plinth than some of the others. She was another Missouri girl, born Elizabeth Grasle in one account and Elizabeth Ruth Grable in another. She was a chorus girl who made her way into films, with a peaches-and-cream complexion glowing healthfully and, after a failed marriage to former child-star Jackie Coogan, was signed up by Twentieth Century-Fox.

She was the star for whom the term Pin-Up Girl might well have been coined. Hers was the photograph inside every G.I.'s locker. And there was, despite all that lovely shaping of flesh and provocative smile over the shoulder, not much that was all that seductive about her. She looked as fresh and uncomplicated as carrot-juice. The titles of her films echoed the remembrance of memories past for millions of soldiers overseas: *Coney Island* and *Sweet Rosie O'Grady* (1943). She could sing a little tune and she could dance a mite more, but she was versatile only in the way her audiences made her versatile. She was a totem for her time.

In 1943 she married the famous trumpeter and bandleader Harry James, and then everything clicked into place. For she seemed utterly and completely like one of those band-singers so popular in the 1930s

and 1940s – girls who stood languidly in front of an orchestra, caressing a microphone and giving forth with a number. She needed that kind of background; her body might have been its own orchestration to others, but as a satisfactory cinematic artist she needed that extension of smooth saxophones and silken strings.

Davis and Crawford

If Grable's emotional location was propping up an orchestra, Bette Davis's was supporting some dud scripts – and scaffolding them so securely that her own conviction sets them like concrete in the mind long after the time when their tawdriness should have

Betty Grable poster for Pin Up Girl putting zip back into the war-time services – and showing off those fabulous legs (TCF, 1944).

87

faded from the memory. She was always aware of her own slightly pop-eyed beauty and knew of other things to distract audiences from too much contemplation of it. One was in a kind of flouncing acting which drew attention to itself as though it were a small boy on a bicycle calling out 'Look, Mom, no hands!'. The other, was a high-toned streak which could convince audiences that she was the one worthy of all the sympathy . . . even if she had just done the foulest of deeds.

It is difficult, for instance, in *The Little Foxes* (1941) not to sit aghast as she watches her husband (Herbert Marshall) fumble for his heart-attack pills without doing anything about it – but her presence and acting bring about an ambiguity within us that makes us recognize her stature and her capacity to withstand the pain of others. She communicated here a star's real quality – of persuading us to go along with her.

Bette Davis took on the wrath and might of Warner Brothers, because of the dire quality of the scripts she had been given – leaving them in the lurch, being put on suspension. Although she lost, the publicity that she brought to the situation of stars at the mercy of uncaring studios ensured that nothing similar would ever happen again in such a way.

If Vivien Leigh could be accused of not having enough extravagance, then Bette Davis might well be fingered as having too much. And yet, such is the world of cinema, that if it works then it works – that is all there is to it. And with Bette Davis, it worked. In spaces. She walked always as though she had a long, heavy velvet train slithering along behind her, which may have been why she was so effective, as the Virgin Queen Elizabeth in *The Private Lives of Elizabeth And Essex* (1939). In her later years she moved into a series of sub-horror movies, after the autumnal sado-masochistic melodrama of *Whatever Happened To Baby Jane* (1962). She said later how much she had enjoyed it and how much she had enjoyed the supposed rivalry that existed with her co-star, Joan Crawford, during the film. 'Joan's a star,' she said. 'You don't quarrel with that kind of star.' She was, of course, very much that kind of star herself.

Joan Crawford, though, was of that type – and yet not of that kind. She was, in all our contemplation of what makes a screen-

goddess, the one who worked the hardest to make herself one. She was determined to become a superstar, no matter how many infirmities of circumstances life might deal out. That she succeeded – and at the cost of the well-publicized hatred of some adopted children – is beyond dispute. She was her own best friend, but ultimately her own worst enemy. She was what Frank Sinatra called Betty Hutton, a yeoman – that is, one who shows the muscles of talent working, who reveals the cogs whirring away inside the machine.

She was the fan-made-incarnate, the girl from the sticks who achieves stardom simply and almost as an act of will. Her audience took to her in the 1930s and more specifically in the 1940s because she was so obviously 'one of them'. She was born with the improbable name of Lucille Le Sueur in Texas of parents who were later to separate and, eventually, got bit parts in movies, especially with MGM. Louis B. Mayer

'Les Grande Dames'. Opposite: Bette Davis in marvellously regal mood, and above, Joan Crawford putting a brave face on it – as always.

Joan Crawford looking suitably menaced by Bette Davis in Whatever Happened To Baby Jane? (*Associates and Aldrich, 1962*).

himself decided that Lucille Le Sueur was not the right sort of name for one of his stars, so a contest was held to decide what she should be called. The contest took place within the pages of a fan-film magazine and the name that came up trumps with the powers-that-be was Joan Crawford which she hated at first. 'It sounded too much like Crawfish. Later I came to love it.'

And she also came to love the way she was treated and groomed at MGM. She said of Mayer: 'I was free to go to him for advice of any kind, any time. He was patient with people, had great judgement and didn't play games. Mr. Mayer always had a magic sense of star material, of personality. He

knew how to build and protect his "properties" and he had a genuine love for them as people . . . .' This may certainly not have accorded with the impressions of other, less impressionable, observers, but Joan Crawford knew which way she wanted her cookie to crumble. Mayer held the keys to the coffers of success that Joan Crawford wanted so desperately to open.

It was *Our Dancing Daughters* (1928) that first made the public aware of Joan Crawford; it was an awareness that she would never let them forget over the next few generations of her stardom. But it is indicative, even at this early stage, just how she realized that her image had to be fos-

Typical of the kind of styles that Joan Crawford made her own trade-mark is this creation by her favourite designer Adrian.

tered, nourished and sustained if it were to have any kind of continuity of impact on people whom she had learned in childhood could be painfully fickle: 'That fall of 1928 I went around with my box camera taking pictures of every marquee that had my name in lights. From this period on, I was never again carefree. Before, I had been absolutely sure of myself in a brash and very young way. Now I began to study and observe myself. I was immersed in my own image on the screen: that will show you how immature I was. But I did have sense enough to know I must work and work hard? I kept setting the goal higher and higher.'

There was a period in the Thirties when Crawford began to imitate Garbo in the way she looked to the camera. Her make-up accentuated her large, soulful eyes, while the cheek hollows were shaded and the mouth smeared with a slash of lipstick. In the meantime she approached the famous MGM dress designer, Adrian, and for her he designed the wide-shouldered costumes that were so much a part of the way she looked – and which were so imitable by shop girls who might well have been called Lucille, but who now wanted to be called Joan.

'Adrian had a profound effect both on my professional and personal life. He put the

Nils Asther and Joan Crawford in Letty Lynton *(1932). Adrian was the designer here too.*

ruffles in the right places and showed me how to dress. Right timing is always important ... Adrian's style timing has always been right. From 1929 to 1943 this creative, resourceful man designed everything I wore in pictures and most of what I wore in my personal life .... In fact I don't remember any fashions before Adrian. My style had been bows 'everywhere. But Adrian toned me down, not just in colour', but in line – and gave me the tailored look that was so distinctive. He decided to emphasize my broad, square shoulders and this became a fashion sensation ...'

In fact Adrian's broad-shouldered appeal came about because of the necessity of de-emphasizing what, in fact, were Crawford's rather large hips. So he hit upon the notion of making her shoulders even broader by enveloping them in a great froth of ruffles for *Letty Lynton* (1932). So, her hips seemed smaller and the dress was adjudged so remarkable that thousands of copies were made and it was chain-stored throughout the world. Said a rather cynical Adrian:

'Who would ever believe that my whole career would rest on Joan Crawford's shoulders!' The comparison with Atlas did not go unremarked among the more classically minded of his customers.

Clothes, of course, help make a goddess; Adrian was one of the most perceptive about what the camera required in the way of good looks. When the face was as good for a camera to gaze upon as was Crawford's or Garbo's, he thought it best to keep the important details of a costume above the waist. So, for instance, for Crawford's work in *Forsaking All Others* (1934), he created a dark coat with a white plate-like collar that extended above and beyond her shoulders. He amplified the idea in her *No More Ladies* (1935) with a vast starched white collar which – as one fashion critic of the time commented – looked like two white sails. It extended so far over her arms that she was unable to get a cigarette to her mouth.

There was a lot of that about – putting meaningful cigarettes to mouths. It filled in the time between the snappy dialogue that

passed for sophistication at that time. To be truthful not all that many Joan Crawford movies at that time were more than brash melodramas in which she excelled in a dominating way that might well make any man quiver at the real-life thought of coming to terms with her in actuality. But by the end of the 1930s and into the 1940s she could well stand her ground with the other studio goddesses. In *The Women* (1939), for instance, from a play by Clare Booth – an all-female account of bitchery triumphant and melodramatic – she was up against other female stars, such as Norma Shearer, Rosalind Russell, Mary Boland, Paulette Goddard, and Auntie Ruth Hussey and all. She managed, though, to get this plaudit from the 'New York Herald Tribune': 'Joan Crawford gives a conventional but striking performance as the shopgirl who tries to hook the heroine's husband.' And the 'New York Times': 'Miss Crawford is hard as nails . . . which is as it should be.'

The 'hard-as-nails' description stuck throughout her career, although it was to be leavened by the realization of sadness for her plight in what might well be the best of her films of her later years, *Mildred Pierce* (1945). Here are the broad shoulders, the resolute, sculpture-planed features. And a story – directed by Michael Curtiz – that, while edging towards a certain women's liberation, was yet of the implicit opinion that a good man was really needed in a woman's life if it were to be at all complete. Here she is pitted unknowingly against another, younger woman (Ann Blyth) who is also her daughter and who drains her of strength and emotion. It was melodrama of the kind to which Crawford could give great emotional value – and she did.

This started a cycle of suffering women which, at times, became almost risible in such movies as *Flamingo Road* (1949) and *This Woman Is Dangerous* (1952). Her cinematic suffering was borne out by her private life. After a series of failed marriages she had adopted four children one of whom, Christine, wrote an exposé book,

'Mommie Dearest', which was later made into a film (1983) with Faye Dunaway in the rôle of a Crawford whose neuroses made her beat her children and insist that bathrooms be scrubbed to a cleanliness even Lady Macbeth would have admired.

Miss Dunaway could not, however hard she tried achieve much in the way of projecting a woman who had become such a self-parody in her later years. The mask of her face was immobile and fixed. Scott Fitzgerald has often been quoted about his time in Hollywood and Joan Crawford: 'She can't change her emotions in the middle of a scene without going through a sort of Jekyll and Hyde contortion of the face . . . .Also, you can never give her such a direction as "telling a lie", because if you did, she would practically give a representation of Benedict Arnold selling West Point to the British.'

But if Joan Crawford was a goddess who, in her latter years, became a travesty, her early ones had at least been years of power and influence. She also had a certain control on the way her worshippers behaved and how they carried themselves, broad-shouldered, through a world which was changing too fast for understanding. Perhaps the bizarre name of Lucille Le Sueur was more appropriate for those strange, queen-bee movies that were her last. That name matches their grotesque emotional stratagems.

Barbara Stanwyck – born Ruby Stevens – another man's woman whose feminine appeal was irresistible.

Stanwyck and Novak

The writer David Thomson has noted similarities between the work of Joan Crawford and that of another woman whose career reached fruition about the same time – Barbara Stanwyck. She, too, did her fair share of cinematic suffering – but she always seemed to have brought some of it upon herself by virtue of the nature of the characters she inhabited. Born Ruby Stevens in Brooklyn she evidently had it tough as a youngster, graduating into the world of burlesque but eventually coming through into some kind of big-time in Hollywood via the movie that was to make her famous, *Ladies Of Leisure* (1930). It was

directed by Frank Capra whose memorable quotation is that: 'She's one of those women one falls in love with at first sight'.

Her roles were never alarmingly spectacular, but there is a momentum to all her work which makes one realize that she was a personality better than all the filmic soap-operas – before the name was invented – and that there was a continuing Stanwyck persona above all their mediocrities. The corn for her was ever-green in such dramas as *Stella Dallas* (1937) or – even more heartwincingly – *Remember The Night* (1940) as a shoplifter.

Her best roles number – in my opinion, anyway – only a couple. That of the eponymous anti-heroine in *The Lady Eve* (1941), Preston Sturges's comedy in which she made Henry Fonda trip the light fantastic in a marvellous *gavotte* of conning and conned. And, of course, there was Billy Wilder's *Double Indemnity* (1944) in which, with blonde wig and ankle-bracelet, she sets out not only to disrupt the whole of Fred MacMurray's morality and life – but her masculine audience as well.

She was, as a goddess, a woman star whose appeal has always been primarily to men – lighting their cigarettes, knocking back drinks with them, throwing them back the repartee which they may have pitched her way. In later years she went into television with such series as 'The Big Valley', which is usually retirement for goddesses. But the small screen could not diminish or tame her own kind of sex appeal. She still had her worshippers . . . who remembered that first shot of her in *Double Indemnity* walking down a staircase with that ankle-bracelet gleaming like avarice upon Fred MacMurray's troubled mind.

Barbara Stanwyck was once quoted in a film-magazine interview as saying about her start in movies: 'I've had to push every gate that was ever opened to me.' That, indeed, is true of many early women stars celebrated here. There is the division between those who had it made and those – you might say – who had to be made before they could have it. Kim Novak was somewhere in between. Perhaps she never quite achieved goddess-status for as long as others herein contemplated, but she made an impact for a time. She was, in her fashion, a woman who was created by men. Her beauty always seemed to embarrass her, because to her it must have seemed ungainly. I met her in her later years when any questions about her early career seemed to be hurtful to her, so that our conversation ended in her tears and my regrets.

She had been dubbed Miss Deepfreeze in a contest when she got a Columbia contract and went into movies such as *The French Line* (1953), *Phffft!* (1954) and then – on loan-out – for *The Man With The Golden Arm* (1956) to play the loving broad trying to bring Frank Sinatra back from his dope-haunted existence to some kind of reality. But one of her most dramatic and luminous performances was to come with Alfred Hitchcock and *Vertigo* (1958). Whatever independence she might have had was sub-

verted by the Master's creation of her into the image he really desired. The fashion designer Edith Head has said that what mattered to Hitchcock was the way his leading ladies looked. He liked *eau de nil* green and greys. 'When we started *Vertigo* I went to Kim Novak's dressing room and she said "Dear Edith, how nice to meet you. I must tell you that the only things I never wear are tailored suits, anything grey and black pumps. My shoes must be hued to match my stockings."'.

Hitchcock told Edith Head not to worry, because the script said that Kim Novak was to wear a grey tailored suit – and black pumps. No more was said on the subject. Kim Novak had given in to the director. She wore what she was told to wear, a grey tailored suit and black pumps.

Kim Novak's fame, though, never lived beyond that of her creators. As a sex-symbol people did not know how to classify her, so she went into an oblivion which she might have found restful after a career which – as she told me – was 'always full of

Hush! Kim Novak wards off an obsessive James Stewart in Alfred Hitchcock's Vertigo *(1958).*

strain'. And, anyway, for the blonde image there was always Marilyn Monroe ... but that was later.

War makes everyone cosmopolitan. And it is intriguing to note how foreign actresses were making themselves felt within the confines of Hollywood. Such a one was Danielle Darrieux who only came to Hollywood to make one film, *The Rage Of Paris* (1938). She was involved in the amorous merry-go-round of Max Ophuls' *La Ronde* (1950) but before that she had made her cinematic presence felt in many films via a persona which suggested an aristocratic background spiced with sexuality. Ms Darrieux was once reported to have said that she was inspired to move from stage to screen 'because of Elizabeth Taylor; she was and is so beautiful that I thought it would be an honour to follow her.' Not that the two ever met – certainly there are no reports of such a meeting – but in contemplating goddesses one must never forget Elizabeth Taylor.

Elizabeth Taylor

Over-indulged – by herself more than anyone – and over-married, Elizabeth Taylor seems at times to have become a parody of what can happen to a movie star once she

Above: Kim Novak puts on her sultry look.

Right: Import Danielle Darrieux does the same.

Opposite: Elizabeth Taylor at the beginning of her sultriness in National Velvet *(MGM, 1944).*

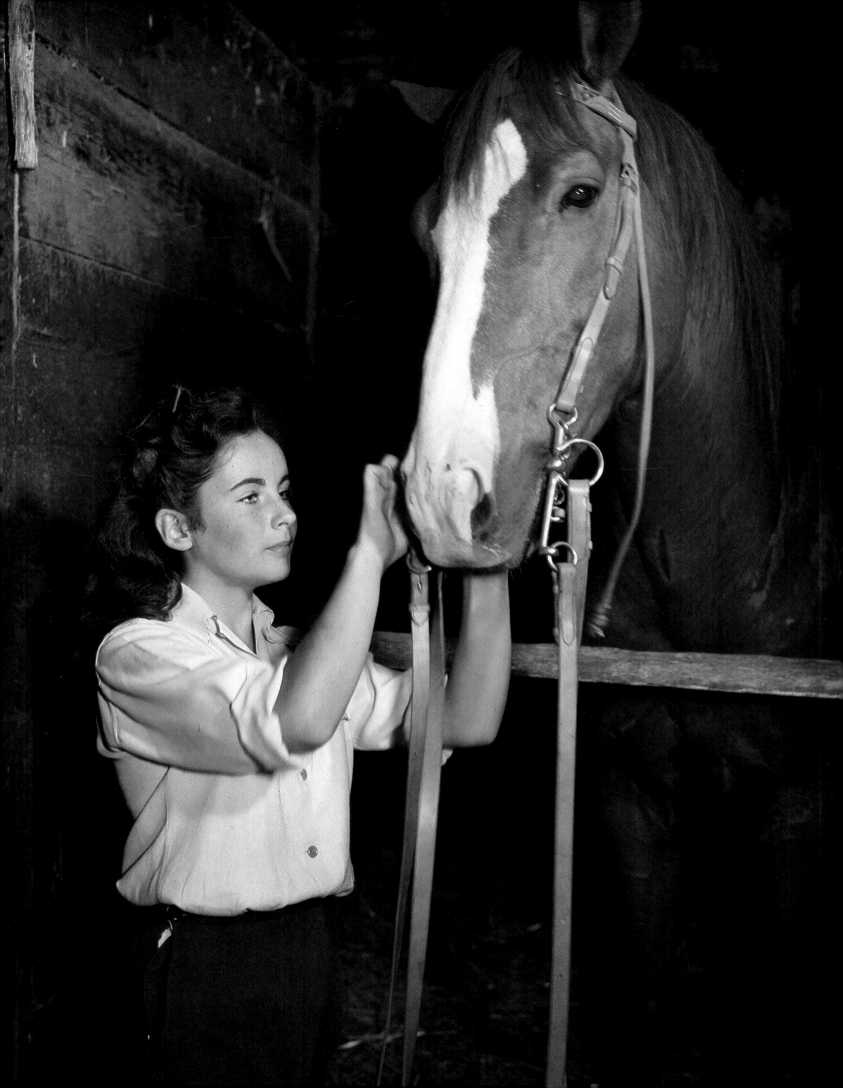

Elizabeth Taylor and Richard Burton at the end of their emotional tether in Who's Afraid Of Virginia Woolf? *(Warner, 1966).*

starts to believe what the publicists write about her. Yet we must always realize that her career and her beauty were as much a part of people's lives as the ice-cream they bought at the interval between movies. Perhaps, her very lushness spoke for a way of picture-going life which now seems lost and gone for ever.

She was a phenomenal child star with such features as *Lassie Come Home* (1943) and later with *National Velvet* (1944) and it was her beauty which radiated advance warning of the talent that was to come. She had a gift for comedy which was never properly utilized, although one wonders if she were, in fact, sending herself up with such dreadful contrivances as *The Mirror Crack'd* (1980), her last film of any note.

There were times when her love-life dominated all the headlines, as though the story of scandals and intrigues and divorces were part of the rich parade of some ancient love goddess. As one cynic remarked: 'Her best acting is kept for the newspapers.' Yet there were movies, such as *Who's Afraid Of Virginia Woolf?* (1966), which showed that she was more than a plumply elegant clothes-horse.

She herself said: 'The Elizabeth Taylor who's famous, the one on celluloid really has no depth or meaning to me. It's a totally superficial working thing . . . a commod-

ity . . . . I have never tried to analyze why so many people go to my movies. I suppose if people stopped buying the commodity and I cared, I would try to figure out what ingredients are missing.'

As a star Elizabeth Taylor seems to have been the most manipulative of all her talents and beauty (we must never forget *that* ingredient of the commodity she spoke about). For a time she was wasted, at MGM, on rather genteel rôles which bestowed her beauty upon the public eye, but seemed to forget that she had a gutsy vitality which could bolster any film beyond the usual limitations of what was being offered to her at the time. Even her flawed foray into the most famous love object of all, *Cleopatra* (1963), saw her as a decorative ornament, although there were times when her innate ability shone through like a watermark.

Elizabeth Taylor's trouble was an unusual one among those women stars who feature in these pages in that her origins were impeccably lush and moneyed. She herself has said: 'I had too much too early.' In that indulgence can be seen the corrupting roots of a bloom which has never flowered into anything at all intellectually substantial. 'I never had it tough like Ava', she is quoted as saying about one of her best friends. In a way that is her loss.

Opposite: Taylor as Maggie The Cat in Cat On A Hot Tin Roof – *with Paul Newman (Avon, 1958).*

Ava Gardner with one of the most aggressive come-hither looks in the business, seen here in Pandora And The Flying Dutchman *(Romulus, 1950). Ernest Hemingway once said she was his favourite woman.*

Ava Gardner

Ava Gardner, though, seems to have had it tough all the way, although she matured into one of the most fabulous beauties of the cinematic century. Ava Gardner is the love goddess who graduated into becoming an earth-mother.

She was born in Smithfield, North Carolina, as Lucy Johnson, one of the six children of a poverty-stricken tenant farmer and, by all accounts, had a childhood as deprived of love as her father's growing-earth was deprived of nutrition. But her brother-in-law was a photographer and sent her photograph to MGM; a screen test followed and she gradually became known. A marriage to Mickey Rooney, quickly followed by divorce, helped her to more public recognition.

Her good looks always suggested that there was some kind of intelligence behind the surface gloss. She appeared in some of the early Dr. Kildare movies – usually as decorative back-up to the drama – but her contract with MGM got her into a whole raft of movies, such as *The Hucksters* (1947), *One Touch Of Venus* (1948) – typecasting? – and the remake of Show Boat (1951), besides the bizarre and exotic *Pandora And The Flying Dutchman* (1950) which had her falling in love with James Mason who, *sans* Wagner, was doomed to perpetual journeyings.

Her movies certainly weren't classics, although after the film of Ernest Hemingway's *The Snows Of Kilimanjaro* (1952) the author himself said that he wished that only she would play the woman in re-creations of his books. It was that simply by being in them she gave them an elegance of distinction which made them different, which set them apart.

She was, in those films, simply made for mink: the tall beauty of her body looked as though it already wore high heels – even if it didn't. That she could act seemed of little importance when compared with the way she *looked*. But she could act as well. As the Anglo-Indian in *Bhowani Junction* (1956) she was touchingly vulnerable, and in John Huston's version of Tennessee Williams' *Night Of The Iguana* (1964) she was earth-maternal in the way of a woman who had loved not wisely but too well – but enjoyed every damned minute of it. She worked again for Huston in *The Life And Times Of Judge Roy Bean* (1972) as the desirable Lily Langtry who is worshipped from afar by Paul Newman as Judge Bean. It seemed to be her destiny in life to be worshipped, although her many marriages – to Mickey Rooney, band leader Artie Shaw and Frank Sinatra – suggested that worship could come unglued in the heat of close-up life. Her personal identification was always, she said, with the adored Lady Brett Ashley in another Hemingway film, *The Sun Also Rises* (1957).

It is an intriguing fact – perhaps helped by the increase in mass circulation of much of the media – that love goddesses and their toings and froings were becoming more and more accepted as emotional currency for the public. Their scandals and passionate vicissitudes were accounted fair – or, rather, unfair – game for any gossip columnist or a journalist wanting to gain a quick and easy headline. Ava Gardner was

Above: Ava as the Russian baroness in 55 Days At Peking *(Samuel Bronston, 1962).*

Left: Ava with an Errol Flynn nearing the end of a boozed life in The Sun Also Rises *(TCF, 1957).*

*Opposite: Not so simply
. . . Rita.*

one of the first of those who seemed to live continually more in the headlines than in her movies. 'I don't know who gets the most publicity – Elizabeth (Taylor) or me. I only know as sure as hell that I don't need it and don't want it.'

To be sure, though, she brought much of it upon herself, by choosing to be seen in all the wrong places; her fascination with bull-fighters and the bull-ring became a notorious subject for any kind of scandal. She was, though, in her way carrying on a kind of tradition. And that was one which had been started by her predecessor in the glamour stakes: Rita Hayworth. Rita Hayworth had forecast that Ava Gardner would be the one who would 'take on my sort of roles, the slinky, sultry type. I wish her luck.'

Rita Hayworth

Luck had everything to do with the rise and fall of Rita Hayworth. Good luck and bad luck. But good luck for audiences, especially in the way she put across the song 'Put The Blame On Mame' in perhaps her most erotic movie, *Gilda* (1946). She is a cousin of Ginger Rogers and her father was a Spanish dancer and her mother a Ziegfeld showgirl (her real name is Margarita Carmen Cansino). Despite early promise at Twentieth Century-Fox she seemed all set for the obscurity of B-pictures until she married a man who was more than twenty years her senior and who set down his own job to pick up hers – to manage her. That

was how she got a contract with Columbia and her hair changed overnight from brunette to auburn.

Her first really interesting role was in *Only Angels Have Wings* (1939) and she followed this with a whole series of movies which exploited her considerable beauty, relying on her now-famous face and figure for their very titles: *You Were Never Lovelier* (1942) and *Cover Girl* (1944). She was – to quote one writer 'the thinking G.I.'s pin-up'. She married Orson Welles whose film *The Lady From Shanghai* (1948) seems almost like a dedication to her – and later eloped with the Aly Khan.

As an actress she was never properly used in the kind of roles that would have kept her afloat in the undoubtedly choppy seas that were the Columbia Studios as run by the megalomaniac boss, Harry Cohn. Her appeal was mainly as a sex symbol and her picture in 'Life' magazine was said to have upped that periodical's circulation by many thousands. Her picture also had the dubious honour of being on the side of the atomic bomb dropped on the Bikini atoll.

Perhaps there was less to Rita Hayworth than met the eye, but there was certainly plenty to meet the eye in the most seductively erotic way possible. There were, though, ways in which that could be manipulated. For instance, the fashion designer Jean-Louis found that when he met her for *Tonight And Every Night* (1945) she was pregnant, so that her version of the samba 'You Excite Me' had to be filmed at the beginning of shooting when she could still, with decency, wear the costume that he had designed for her – which had a bare midriff. There was also a lot of trouble, he recalled, with the red of the costume matching the red of Hayworth's hair. 'We couldn't have a real red; it had to be muddy with an umber dye.' He had problems of a similar nature with *Gilda* with Hayworth's 'Put The Blame On Mame' number, in which she stripped off her elbow-length gloves as she sang, which was shot soon after the birth of her daughter Rebecca.

Certainly, Hayworth was a product of the studios that created her, but the sadness is that she was never allowed to exert her talents within that system. But manufactured or not Rita Hayworth never came even close to the exploitation that was lavished upon another of our love beings – Jane Russell.

Below: Rita Hayworth putting the fabulous blame on Mame in Gilda *(Columbia, 1946).*

Jane Russell survived many insults, such as the title of the film in which she starred with Frank Sinatra and Groucho Marx: Double Dynamite *(aka* It's Only Money, *produced 1948. RKO 1951).*

Jane Russell

Here was a woman for whom a parody of the song 'Thanks For The Mammary' might well have been written. Her thirty-eight-inch bust was both cause of amusement and envy, but its reputation gave her a kind of notoriety which made it hard to discern that there was actually a person with skill hiding away in the headlines.

She was, in the 1940s, with the film *The Outlaw* (1943) a woman whose image it was hard to get away from – if you had wanted to, that is. A poster, showing her with ample cleavage leaning back invitingly against what looked like a haystack was everywhere. Hers was indeed a treasure chest and her performances, while enlarging – if possible – on that fact, do show that she had a certain cynical enjoyment of her own position as sex symbol.

How she became that sort of symbol is one of those stories of luck and coincidence which enhance the rags-to-riches stories on which Hollywood and showbusiness thrive. She was a chiropodist's assistant when a friend sent a photograph of her to the millionaire recluse Howard Hughes who was, as was reported so often, also an engineer as well as a businessman besides being interested in movies. Sensing possibilities, like a pointer-dog of gossip sniffing fair game, he realized that Miss Russell's two attributes were her two major assets. He designed a specially-cantilevered brassière for her and put her into *The Outlaw*. It is a Western that is memorable only for the appearance of Jane Russell who – realizing the strange position in which she found herself – took whatever movies there were around, even if they did contain ruthless single-entendres in the title (*Double Dynamite*, 1951, was one of them).

'I have learned to live with my breasts', she is quoted as saying, and there is a certain amused relish in that remark. Certainly she had learned to live with the kind of introduction made by comedian Bob Hope who, at a stage show, said: 'And now here is the two and only Jane Russell'. She appeared with Bob Hope in a spoof Western, *The Son Of Paleface* (1952), as a gun-toting Calamity Jane character and proved, again, that she was not backwards at coming forward and making fun of herself and her situation. Her bigness proved an advantage in such musicals as *Gentlemen Prefer Blondes* (1953) and *Gentlemen Marry Brunettes* (1955), for it allowed her to stand out among all the other stars (who included Marilyn Monroe).

It was her lot in later movies to be regarded as 'a dame', but she was a pretty classy dame come to that. She was good enough, in 1971, to replace Elaine Stritch as the star of the Broadway musical, 'Company', and in later years appeared in TV commercials extolling bras for 'the fuller figure'. It seemed an inevitable destination and one which her sceptical attitude to life might well have appreciated.

Gentlemen prefer brunettes – or at any rate, Jane Russell.

Doris Day

A spectacular bosom, however, was not as we have seen the only way to become a screen deity. A spectacular way with a certain style of movies could also elevate an actress to that ascendancy. The title of this chapter, about virgins, might well have been written with Doris Day in mind, because the compact blonde that she was – and, hopefully, still is – kept to movies which were romantic comedies hinting at sexual surrender, but she nevertheless kept herself pure until the ultimate in good taste – a bed that had been sanctified by marriage. In *Young At Heart* (1954) she could happily sing that she was 'Ready, Willing and Able' – but the plots of her films gave a reverse thrust to whatever masculine ardour was about to be imposed upon her.

Doris Day – *née* Kappelhoff – specialized in the homespun and, in the late Forties and early Fifties, that was just what audiences wanted. She had the well-scrubbed look that came with much soap and water, a

sprinkle of freckles, and the sort of warmth that returning soldiers would find marvellously welcome. The apple-pie was in the oven and Doris was in bed (but only if it were a marriage bed!).

She made thirty-nine films in a career which spanned twenty years and which started when she was spotted by director Michael Curtiz, singing in a night-club. He gave her a rôle in *Romance On The High Seas* (1948) and then followed that with *Young Man With A Horn* (1950) and – more interestingly – *Storm Warning* (1950). This last was a scarifying account of small-town racism and Doris Day's Nordic blonde cuteness was paradoxically cast as a girl fighting injustice – against members of the Ku Klux Klan who might well have regarded her looks as the norm to which every American should aspire. Her co-star in that movie, Steve Cochran, once told me: 'She was the goddammest professional to work with; she was always on time and on cue, and, even though she was fairly new to the

business, she knew exactly how to upstage you without seeming to mean to. You'd think she was hardly there and then you'd look at the rushes the next day – and realize that Day had done it again. She was right up there in front of the camera. That is who you looked at!'

Her favoured films, though, were the Warner musicals which ranged from *It's A Great Feeling* (1949) to *Lullaby of Broadway* (1951) and, almost inevitably, *Calamity Jane* (1953). She has, in recent years, been claimed oddly by the Women's Lib. movement. For a British National Film Theatre celebration of her movies Jane Clarke and Diana Simmonds wrote about the girl who was so often termed 'the girl next door' or 'the constant virgin': '. . . Day is misremembered as the quintessential Fifties virgin next door which, after a decade of the cult of permissiveness, is anathema in 1980. However, we think the

Day image functions in quite the reverse way. First, the range of performances Day brought to rôles which were often deliberate re-workings of a successful formula. Second, that many of her rôles are particularly relevant today in pre-figuring a less repressive sexuality.'

'Day frequently plays an independent/ working woman who confronts the male and forces him to modify his attitudes and behaviour. Moreover, saying "no" to manipulative sexual situations (a favourite plot device in the sex comedies) is not the same as clinging to one's virginity. Day was offered the part of Mrs. Robinson in *The Graduate*. She turned it down because of its exploitative depiction of sexual relations – an acute assessment which many would now share. So, we challenge you to leave the cinema with your preconceptions intact: lift the winter gloom, be exhilarated and re-remember Doris Day before she was a virgin.' I'm sure the audience had a great time.

It is, though, as the Virgin Goddess that Doris Day is remembered, even if she did move into other acting areas, such as drama, when she took part in Hitchcock's remake of his own *The Man Who Knew Too Much* (1955) or being terror-haunted for *Midnight Lace* (1960), or, even, a more sophisticated comedy than either she, or her audience, were used to, as with *Send Me No Flowers* (1964). She was always a presence to brighten the screen and illuminate the heart with her high-spirits. Her early retirement, after the death of her husband – Martin Melcher, who produced many of her movies – left the cinema a less exuberant place.

Betty Hutton

One can hardly mention Doris Day without, of course, mentioning Betty Hutton – that other blonde bombshell. She, too, touched the spangled West, as did Doris Day with *Calamity Jane*, when she 'made *Annie Get Your Gun* (1950) turning

The rumbustious Betty Hutton as Annie Oakley in Annie Get Your Gun *(MGM, 1950). Gun-toting, fun-toting . . . .*

IN THE MORNING
PHONE THE OFFICE
WE WILL DELIVER
THE MORNING PAPER
~~and HOT COFFEE~~ FREE
with compliments of
The HONEYMOON MOTEL

Betty Hutton in Preston Sturges's The Miracle Of Morgan's Creek – *as the girl who is given a 'pregnant pause for thought' (Paramount, 1943).*

six-shooters into sex-shooters by the force of her personality which was dynamic enough to light up a whole town by the force of her energy-charge. But there was always, where Betty Hutton was concerned, a certain feeling of hysteria as opposed to high spirits, of frenzy where fun would have been more appropriate.

She was another of those who reached the heights from beginnings which were less than auspicious. Born Betty June Thornburg in Battle Creek, Michigan, she sang on street corners as a child to support the family after her father had died. She graduated to big bands when only a teenager and then went to Hollywood. For her Hollywood and the opportunities it offered were very much *The Greatest Show On Earth* (1952) and when I met her she said: 'Hollywood was all to me and so was Paramount Studios; they were family. The

kind of family I never had. I always knew I had talent, but it was Hollywood that ultimately brought it out in me – and gave me a chance.' Her most rewarding and fulfilling film was for director Preston Sturges, *The Miracle Of Morgan's Creek* (1944) in which she played an unmarried girl who gives birth to multiple babies.

Her own private life was not so fruitful. Married and divorced five times, she sank into bankrupted obscurity from which only newspaper headlines were able to rescue her by noting that she had received sustained psychiatric treatment. It was a sad way for a blonde bombshell to disintegrate – not with a bang but a whimper.

But blonde bombshells of her kind were, as a matter of time and *mores*, fading away fast anyway. For there was a new blonde on the horizon, looming like a seductive thunderstorm. Her name was Marilyn Monroe.

The Goddess Image

Vanguard of the Sexual Revolution: Monroe and Bardot

It is not just because the final syllables of their names pronounce a pouting 'O' of invitation that I link these two goddesses to form the basis for this chapter. It is that both Marilyn Monroe and Brigitte Bardot, together and separately, caused a kind of revolution in the goddess-stakes. Their sexual symbolism affected a whole generation and ensured that future creatures of such feminine allure were affected by the attitudes created and inspired by them. After them, nothing would be the same again.

They were stars of such uncompromising brightness that, for a time, they blinded the public into seeing nobody else but them. Not only in imitation of fashions and looks, but their attitude to sex itself can be noted as being among those whose enjoyment of sex – on the screen, anyway – was frank and unashamed. Monroe used the age-old tricks of being pursued by a man until she had got him where she wanted him. Bardot was nakedly without artifice – she not only loved, she lusted.

Both, though, for all the combined impact they had on audiences, came from totally different backgrounds. Bardot was the daughter of wealthy, middle-class parents, while Monroe had an unhappy childhood shadowed by her illegitimacy and a desperate need for money. She was never to forget those years. And there can be detected within her performances a vulnerability, a little girl lost, which adds to the naïve sexiness which only she could communicate with such disturbing skill.

Marilyn Monroe

Many books and mental post-mortems have tried to examine and make clear the way the American dream died within Marilyn Monroe's life. We need not go into the subject as deeply as that, for we are concerned with the immediate impact of her allure – why she so influenced those who came to regard her as a love goddess.

Her childhood and teenage life have been well documented – not least by the present author – but Marilyn enjoyed covering up the tracks that had led her to the pinnacled heights of film-fame. What we do know is that she was born Norma Jean Mortenson in Los Angeles and her mother was a film cutter at Columbia and RKO Studios. Her mother's name was Baker which is why she is often called Norma Jean Baker in some accounts. Yet another woman star in search of a father-figure, Marilyn's early life was burdened by the fact that her mother was often confined in mental institutions, so Marilyn was farmed out to a series of foster homes and she was in an orphanage for two years. She became a paint sprayer in a munitions factory and an Army photographer discovered her looks. Soon, she was a cover girl; soon she was photographed nude (stills later used to embarrass her); soon she was in Hollywood as an actress. Perhaps 'actress' is a misnomer, for she was touted as one of that species of 'starlet' who are seen at premières and receptions – but never, actually, in films. She had been signed to a contract with Twentieth Century-Fox at $125 a week and her name was changed to Marilyn Monroe.

She appeared in publicity pin-ups, got gossiped about in all the right columns and, in 1948, made a movie: *Scudda-Hoo! Scudda-Hay!* She was later dropped by Fox, but was then signed up by Columbia. Again and again she was cast as a rather dizzy platinum blonde before making *The Asphalt Jungle* (1950) and *All About Eve*

The flaunting posture of Marilyn Monroe belies the near-tenderness with which she was adored by millions. As a fantasy figure she was at once Snow White and Cinderella and all the little girls who shouldn't stay out late at night.

114

Early days for Marilyn in Scudda-Hoo! Scudda-Hay! (*GB title:* Summer Lightning, *TCF, 1948).*

Below: Marilyn and Keith Anders in Fritz Lang's Clash By Night (*RKO, 1952).*

(1950). By then she had developed her cute posterior-wiggle and a way of looking from under her eye-lashes which was to become famous, not to say notorious. Her sexiness was always mingled with a kind of innocence, which is what made it so attractive. Director Fritz Lang got her to play the young wayward wife in *Clash By Night* (1952) and later he said: 'She was a very peculiar mixture of shyness and uncertainty ... but she knew exactly how she could affect men.'

There seems to have been little rhyme or reason to the kind of movies that Fox – she was now re-established with them – pushed her into: *Don't Bother To Knock* (1952); *Niagara* (1952); and *There's No Business Like Showbusiness* (1954). But she was collecting a hugely appreciative following – besides husbands and love affairs – and was notably a star. 'Which is what,' she once told me, 'I always wanted to be.'

When she appeared in *The Seven Year Itch* (1955) she was, in fact, playing a fantasy figure, who looked like Marilyn Monroe – because that was the way all female fantasy figures were supposed to look. It was part of her seeming naïvety that she would try to brush up and hold on to the culture for which, she said later, she yearned when she was younger. So she went into *The Prince And The Show Girl* (1957)

Marilyn as the no-better-than-she-should-be Rose in Niagara *(TCF, 1952).*

Beauty and The Brains. Marilyn with Arthur Miller, who wrote The Misfits *for her.*

with Laurence Olivier – who made the mistake of asking her to 'Look sexy' – and later married the American playwright Arthur Miller, therein enshrining the bond between showbusiness and art in a way that the great American public could truly understand. He wrote *The Misfits* (1960) for her, but by then the romance had died on both of them. Before that had come *Some Like It Hot* (1959) for director Billy Wilder, which had her as the vocalist in a girls' band, slightly tipsy, always comic . . . and always touching.

Her reputation for lateness and unprofessionalism on set was nearly as vast as her screen deification. Tony Curtis, on *Some Like It Hot*, was angry enough to say that kissing Marilyn was like kissing Hitler. The director Billy Wilder was asked in an interview if he would go through the whole thing again and confessed: 'I have discussed this with my doctor and my psychiatrist and they tell me I'm too old and too rich to go through this again.'

But the consensus was that she was more sinned against in life than she was sinning

Overleaf: Tom Ewell and Marilyn in the fantasy The Seven Year Itch *(TCF, 1955).*

117

Marilyn and dragsters Jack Lemmon and Tony Curtis in Some Like It Hot *(Mirisch, 1959). Here, her temperament really took off.*

in her career. And in 1962, when she died – on a Saturday night – much of the sympathy that flooded over her resulted from the feeling that, despite all her success and her good looks, she had had a raw deal.

She had worked at Lee Strasberg's Method Studio in an attempt to reconstruct and restructure her acting, and it was Strasberg who gave her funeral eulogy: 'In her own lifetime she created a myth of what a poor girl from a deprived background could attain. For the entire world she became a symbol of the eternal feminine . . . .

'This quality was even more evident when she was on stage. I am truly sorry that the public who loved her did not have the opportunity to see her as we did, in any of the roles that foreshadowed what she would

have become. Without a doubt she would have been one of the really great actresses of the stage.'

What-ifs abound over Marilyn Monroe's career. What if she had had a father? What if her mother had been sane? What if Fox had treated her better in her early days? None of them explain why Marilyn Monroe became so much part of the public consciousness, why every wiggle of her bottom, every move of her mouth was considered important. It is my contention that Marilyn Monroe gave sexuality a human face. If that sounds paradoxical, consider that cinema sex of the goddess variety had, through its existence, been suffering or sentimental or strident. It was high romance or low sensuality. Of course, there were such stars as Garbo who were only too human in their tragedies of love, but there was about Marilyn Monroe a comic poignancy. It was as though her private life – lived amid a gymnasium of hang-ups – had seeped into that public image witnessed by millions. Love wasn't a thing which sacrificed you on the altar of its expediency; you could live to love another day. But, nevertheless, in parting there was some hurt to be felt, some pain to be endured.

It was, people realized, the way it was in real life. To that extent then she was the goddess of the ordinary, of the way people really went about their everyday business. She told me: 'I sometimes wonder why it all happened to me, but it happened after all. You have to count your blessings.'

Marilyn in pensive mood. There was, after all, a lot to worry her.

Above: Arletty with the heavy mysterious femininity which made Le Jour Se Lève *so memorable (Daybreak. Sigma, 1939).*

Opposite: Simone Signoret as she appeared in Jack Clayton's film of Room At The Top *(Remus, 1958).*

French Goddesses

The blessings bestowed upon Brigitte Bardot were many and varied from an early age and she used them to assemble her sexual technique with magnificent ferocity and organization. She was the original of a long line of child-women who were to come from France, from Françoise Arnoul to Dany Robin via Cécile Aubry. Her understanding of the needs of men was powerful and implicit in the sway of her body, the swing of her thighs. She was in a stark contrast with many of the French women who had become goddesses in their own country if not in the world. Previously, French women stars, such as Michèle Morgan, relied on a heavy-lidded dignity. Their carriage indicated that they might be partners in the act of sex, and never passive, but they still retained a certain physical dignity. Bar-

dot's aura radiated her own needs and heat and it generated a similar desire among men.

It is worthwhile, to understand that contrast, to realize the kind of star who held sway in France until Bardot broke through the veil. Such a star, for example, was Arletty, whose mysterious femininity stirred thousands of young English boys studying French for the examinations to realize that this was one enormous reason to conjugate irregular verbs with some dexterity in case one went to France and met her.

Born Arlette-Léonie Bathiat she made no films until 1930 when she was in a movie called *Un Chien Qui Rapporte*. Thereafter she was in much demand by the director Marcel Carné and the writer Jacques Prévert, both of whom obviously saw in her beauty an echo of the sad fatalism that was evident in some of the films that they made, such as *Le Jour Se Lève* (1939) and *Les Enfants du Paradis* (1944).

Her looks were luminous and yet they illuminated not the looker, but her own soul. She hinted at more, perhaps, than could be delivered and yet she became the epitome of what French movies could be all about.

After her there was Simone Signoret, whose expression may have been more open but who still had that same dignity of movement and way of holding herself which seems entirely appropriate to the Continental goddesses of that time. It seems almost like Signoret speaking when in the British *Room At The Top* (1958) she accuses the social climbing Laurence Harvey of treating her as though she were a dirty postcard. Saucy, Simone certainly wasn't; sexy, yes.

For a woman so French, though, she came in fact from Wiesbaden in Germany and was born with the surname Kaminker. Now, she is more plump than pretty but then she was the idol of every good director's eye, working with Max Ophuls as the hooker in *La Ronde* (1950), with H.G. Clouzot on *The Fiends* (1955) and on *Evil Eden* (1956) for Luis Buñuel. She was always a woman for whom men were supposed to die. Her love had that price to be paid, as in Jacques Becker's marvellous evocation of last-century French life, *Casque d'Or* (1952). She and her husband Yves Montand have espoused radical politics for a great length of time. She once explained

Signoret in the 1952 movie Casque d'Or (*aka* Golden Marie).

Opposite: Bardot as we created her.

to me that that was why she worked so hard and made so many films (her work-rate was phenomenal) – she wanted to put money into 'The Cause'. One hopes that 'The Cause' did not forget when she grew old not all that gracefully and films seemed harder to come by. This, then, was the class of actress whom Bardot was to break through with her pertness and provocative manner which seemed to know no shame.

Brigitte Bardot

Bardot's body was and is a delight for photographers and there is an apocryphal story about the cameramen on 'Paris Soir' and Bardot. If they had contributed some unusually good assignment they were given a token of esteem by being sent to photograph Bardot.

In his book, 'Bébé: The Films of Brigitte Bardot', the writer Tony Crawley wrote with some perception about the girl who

was supposed to have been created by Roger Vadim: 'Brigitte Bardot is no creation – more a recreation. No manufactured, Svengali dream-wish fulfilment, not of Vadim, nor anyone else. She is a state of mind, body and spirit. An attitude of mind, as critic Raymond Durgnat specified; and a delight in ours. A product not entirely rare, of her time – not ours. Of Paris under the Nazi heel, of the Occupation and the preoccupation with treacherous Vichy politicking, black-market bitterness and the post-'45 French youthful delight in slick American commercialism. In order to sell by demand, first a demand has to be created – and *that* is where Roger Vadim strolled in. With him, and in the company of several like-minded attitudinists the lucidly amoral, splendidly disdainful creature to be labelled BB was already self-established before Vadim drew it into the light of cinema projection.'

Bardot has said: 'I'm a Brigitte Bardot. And that Brigitte Bardot – the one I see in the magazines and the newspapers, the one up there on the screen – that Brigitte will never, for example, be sixty years of age.'

A goddess then, to realize her own godhead and her own immortality. Age could not wither at all the first fine careless rapture of our understanding of the kind of image which she projected on to the screen. She was, even after leaving Vadim, aware that she had been manufactured to a certain extent. As Crawley said, she came from a world which had grown sick of the hangovers of wartime. She cut through that blur of compromise with her own uncompromising body. Unlike Marilyn Monroe she was totally self-conscious. Her life may

be seen as following through a blueprint which had been mapped out very early on.

At first the blueprint was Vadim's, who released her from what she later called her 'bourgeois prison'. It was, despite those jail terms, a rather attractive middle-class family with some considerable wealth. Vadim's realization of Bardot was: 'I wasn't immediately sexually aroused: for me, you have to have something to look forward to in sex. I do not like women who are totally aware of their beauty or their looks. There is nothing less sexy than a woman who knows what effect she has on a man.'

'Two things struck me about her, then. First, her style. She had a way to be very free with her body. And her mind. When I say free with her body, I'm talking about

the way she will walk, move, look at people, sit. She was a fantastic classic dancer – and she had the sort of grace and elegant movement that good, classic dancers have. She was also, for a little *bourgeoise*, in a certain way very revolutionary. She will approach life, any kind of problem, with a really free mind, which was interesting. And she had a very good sense of dialogue. Just a few words – and she was on the point. Great spontaneity. That is one reason for her success . . . .' She recalled later that her legs helped, too, and her bosom. She was always very much *aware* – of herself and her effect on other people, especially men.

She made a number of small films in the early days, including one for the Rank Organization in Britain called *Doctor At Sea* (1955), which had her teasing a rather bewildered-looking Dirk Bogarde. But international acclaim – if not notoriety – really came with *And God Created Woman* (1956), which revealed her as Juliette, a girl who, as Vadim, her director, said 'is of today and to whom the taste of pleasure is neither limited by morals or social taboos. In pre-war literature and cinema one would have painted her simply as a whore. Here she is a very young woman without, of course, any excuses save for those of the heart.' Nude sunbathing and a dance that was supposed to throw all caution to the winds – and men to the wolves of desire – were the principal set-pieces of Vadim's movie. It looks curiously dated today and naïve.

Bardot and Dirk Bogarde in the British film she made for the Rank Organization, Doctor At Sea *(Group Films, 1955).*

127

Reeling, writing and the arithmetic was box-office returns for Bardot in And God Created Woman. *A strip-off sensation (aka* And Woman . . . Was Created. *UCIL/ Cocinar, 1956).*

Whatever merits the movie now has – and, all things considered, they are not many – it certainly elevated Bardot to a kind of stardom. The Roman Catholic Legion of Decency found it 'an open violation of Christian and traditional morality'. 'Time' magazine was a little more discreet, saying that the film 'opens with a shot that promises a good deal more than the picture delivers. There lies Brigitte, stretched out from end to end of the Cinemascope screen, bottoms up and bare as a censor's eyeball. In the hard sun of the Riviera, her round little rear glows like a peach, and the camera lingers on the subject as if waiting for it to ripen . . . .'

And ripen it did over a succession of films designed specifically to exploit that body and that reputation. The turning point came with a film called *En Cas De Malheur* (1958) in which, for the first time, she was cast with one of the great actors of the French cinema (hitherto, they had been youngsters like herself) – Jean Gabin. He was reported to have become angry when the subject of working with Bardot was mentioned: 'What? With that girl who goes around naked!' He was, though, convinced. And the story of an aged lawyer falling for the sexual charms of a client who has no other way to pay than by her body became some sort of success – and proved that Bar-

Courtroom drama with Bardot in La Vérité *(The Truth, 1960).*

dot could work with actors more experienced than herself.

After that came *The Truth* (1960) in
which she worked for the great director
Henri-Georges Clouzot and revealed herself as some sort of tragedienne, although
sex was still the underswell of that tragic
flow. For her it was and remained her
favourite film: 'Very important to me. I can
act in it.' Some critics were not so favour-
ably inclined. Bosley Crowther of the 'New
York Times' said: 'The truth about a so-
called Crime Of Passion is what (Clouzot) is
supposed to be trying to fathom . . . but a
viewer might easily get the notion that what
he is really out to do is crowd the screen
with the scorching sensuality of his star performer . . . .' And the film-makers were
creating Brigitte Bardot.

The best directors were always interested
in Bardot in the days when she was becom-

ing as much a myth of France and as legendary and obstinate in her way as Charles De
Gaulle. Her pertness, freshness and
unabashed sexuality marked her as the first
of the liberated women, before the term
Women's Lib. had been coined. Far more
than Marilyn she seemed to enjoy her own
success, despite unfounded rumours of a
couple of attempted suicides over which the
world's press shed a few crocodile tears –
and duly reported.

Almost without seeming to, Brigitte had
arrived at her legend at about the same time
as the new wave of film directors, founded
by contributors to the famed critical
magazine 'Cahiers du Cinéma'. So it was,
perhaps inevitable, that she should have
been involved in filming for the most
famous of such movie-makers, Jean-Luc
Godard. This was for a film called *Le Mépris*
(1963), roughly translated as 'Mistrust' and

Just a couple of old-fashioned girls ... Bardot and Jeanne Moreau in Louis Malle's Viva Maria *(Artistes Associés/Vides, 1965). They actually liked each other.*

Bardot played the bored, sexually unsatisfied wife of a screenwriter (Michel Piccoli) who is trying to finish off a script for Fritz Lang and falling foul of the producer (Jack Palance) and his own existentialist nature.

In 'The Films of Brigitte Bardot' the novelist Alberto Moravia described it as 'the psychological evolution of a couple divided by misunderstanding, first hesitant, fragile, then ultimately irreparable. The wife has contempt for the husband without really understanding why. This contempt, perhaps without sound basis, brings tragic consequences.' Said Bardot afterwards: 'Godard was really scared, you know. Me, too. He came to see me; we called each other Monsieur Godard and Mademoiselle Bardot ....' Nevertheless, that stand-offishness brought about one of the most interesting movies in which Bardot was to find herself; it showed that the break from Vadim – they had been drifting irrevocably apart for some time – was, as in the film, now final.

She was by now so internationally well-known that she could play herself in a rather dismal comedy called *Dear Brigitte* (1965), an American film made in France with James Stewart as the father of an eight-year-old mathematical genius-boy (Billy Mumy) who is also mad about Brigitte Bardot – the libido matures early in this sort of American movie. It was her thirty-sixth screen appearance and the reviews were predictably bad. Wrote Patrick Gibbs in the London 'Daily Telegraph': 'nothing in my memory is so embarrassing as this.'

Brigitte was picked up again by the crest of the New Wave, this time for a more commercially viable proposition than *Le Mépris*. *Viva Maria* (1965) made for another New Wave director, Louis Malle, co-starred her with Jeanne Moreau, another kind of film-star altogether. (Incidentally, the fact that I have not included Moreau among my list of goddesses is not through any disaffection for her on my part. But I do feel that, intelligent and great actress that she is, she has not illumined a segment of legend in the way that the other women in this book have.)

The press, naturally enough, seized upon a possible rivalry between the two Frenchwomen in the film which was an *esprit* about two Marias becoming involved in revolution in Central America at the turn of the century.

The wide-open spaces of Brigitte Bardot in the wide-open spaces of Shalako. *The other cow-puncher is Sean Connery (Dimitri de Grunwald, 1968).*

But Bardot put it in this simple, charming and probably completely fabricated way: 'I like Jeanne very much. Perhaps you could say we are two aspects of the ideal woman. I hardly knew her until the film was proposed. Then we dined together, listened to songs together and hit it off immediately.' Kenneth Tynan, though, writing in the London 'Observer' was not so happy with the result: 'The film suffers from a central invalidating flaw; it entirely fails to justify its basic gimmick, the casting of Dionysiac Bardot opposite Appollonian Moreau. There's hardly any plot conflict between them and the expected confrontation simply does not take place: the script would be much the same if the two parts were rolled into one .... Their routines together, despite anything you may have heard to the contrary, are no anthology-items but self-conscious fiascos, of the sort that you politely applaud at charity matinees. The number in which Bardot "invents" strip-tease is especially contrived; her costume splits quite implausibly, and the subsequent stripping is minimal and sadly unteasing .... A big opportunity has been fumbled.'

Certainly the film does live down to quite a few of Tynan's strictures, although it is not – in retrospect – as bad as all that. Bardot has said that they were two aspects of the same ideal woman. And it takes one to know one!

Bardot made another film for Godard, *Masculin-Féminin* (1965), which he described as 'not a dissertation on youth or even analysis ... but it is a piece of music, a "concerto on youth ...." I wanted, it seems to me, to use cinema to speak of youth, or else I wanted to use youth to speak of cinema .... For me, cinema is at the same time, life. It is something that photographs life.'

Comfort me! Lana Turner beseeches John Gavin in Imitation Of Life, *a Douglas Sirk weepie of a special kind (U-I, 1959).*

The idea of the bedroom-eyed Bardot out in the great wide open spaces – revealing, perhaps the wide open spaces of her body – was one that appealed to film-makers. *Shalako* (1968) was one of those which drew her out into New Mexico to encounter Sean Connery and Stephen Boyd and to give her the unlikely name of the Countess Irina Lazaar. She said: 'I have never made a cowboy picture. I like to try something new.'

It seemed that newness and novelty was all in the attempt to present the image of Brigitte Bardot in a different way. Not many of them were successful, as for instance *If Don Juan Were A Woman* (1973) a Franco-Italian extravaganza by a returned Vadim which posited the idea of her as Jeanne, insatiably immoral and putting her – at one point – into bed with another woman, Jane Birkin. Who needed it? Certainly not Brigitte Bardot who was only destroying her own myth by the kind of tosh with which she was becoming associated in her later films.

Perhaps, she realized this, which may account for her virtual retirement – apart from interesting TV interviews, carefully rigged by her staff – and her absorbed involvement with wildlife conservation.

She herself was a wild creature, whom not even the harsh reality of films could tame. She did herself no good as a goddess with many of her films. But she surmounted even them. She had one thing to elevate her, an almost unconscious springboard – the sense of her own style. That was what the world recognized.

Lana Turner

The historian John Kobal writes that the era of the Love Goddess virtually ended with the death of Monroe in 1962, a fact of death which seems to me to be in dispute. Certainly, publicity was needed more to

promote the goddess image, but the result could well be pretty much the same, as for instance with Lana Turner, whose well-stacked sweaters gave her the title of 'Sweater Girl' and who made a kind of mark via such films as *Johnny Eager* (1941), *The Postman Always Rings Twice* (1946) and *The Flame And The Flesh* (1954). Certainly, the publicity about her was much and profound. It even seemed that the real-life drama concerning her and gangster Johnny Stompanato might well have been created by some over-the-top publicist, because when she returned to the movies after the court uproar – that had involved her daughter in some unfounded allegations – she was much in demand, especially by producer Ross Hunter, and made *Imitation Of Life* (1959) which had her lush and plush and every woman's daydream in a story of high romance if, unfortunately, rather low morals.

But if publicists could make goddesses, then so, too, could film-makers themselves. And so we return to Roger Vadim.

Jane Fonda

As I have said, Vadim had directed the movie about Bardot as a Don Juan and it is an odd thought that Vadim was both responsible for Bardot, the first of the implicitly liberated ladies, and then of the articulately liberated goddess, Jane Fonda herself. He was, of his voyeuristic kind, a goddess-maker extraordinaire . . . .

He was very much of his Swinging Sixties time. Born Roger Vadim Plemiannikov in Paris of Ukrainian-French descent he realized – perhaps unconsciously – that there was now a public appetite for a sex which was of the time. And the time thought that it was the most candid and daring that there had ever been. Permissive was the word that was just beginning to be bruited around and talked about. There was, in the general philosophical air, a tendency to think about thought when it came to sex. Oh, yes, Vadim was very much of that time.

Jane Fonda, the daughter of Henry and the sister of Peter, married Vadim in France and made some all-too-revealing movies for him, including his version of *La Ronde* (1964) and *La Curée* (1966). Then there was the sexual strip cartoon of *Barbarella* (1967) in which she looks amazingly energetic as well as sensual.

Fonda is, of her kind, a sort of sanitized goddess, but she was too intellectually aggressive in later life to stay in the rôle of passive sexual dumbness which Vadim seemed to want for her. And, anyway, his 'discoveries' after Bardot all seemed to be simulacrums of the original. Jane Fonda was not really in the likeness of that image. Her image was to be fully realized later, when she married radical Tom Hayden and her liberal instincts were transformed into the kind of left-wing consciousness that could make Richard Nixon reach for his recording-tapes.

Vadim's later goddesses were nowhere in the same category as Bardot or Fonda, although Annette Stroyberg came close to what must have been his ultimate ideal.

Opposite: Lana Turner contemplating life as she had lived it.

Below: Jane Fonda, before aerobics took over, with Peter McEnery in Vadim's La Curée *(aka* The Game Is Over, *1966).*

137

For, the truth has to be that if Vadim had created Bardot, then Bardot herself had created Vadim. Without him she somehow or other discovered the goddess within her. Without her he would never have been a major creative force.

Deneuve, Christie and Vitti

It will be noted that in this chapter on 'Monroe and Bardot' I am stowing away other goddesses. That is because M and B seemed to usher in a whole new species of woman star. Like, for instance, Catherine Deneuve who, although she had a child by Vadim never got herself tethered in marriage to him. She did, however, make at least one film with him, *Vice And Virtue* (1962), which was based on the Marquis de Sade's 'Justine'.

There is something about Deneuve's passive, blonde beauty which does seem to show up the kinks in a film director's sexual armour, considering that, for Luis Buñuel she appeared in two of his best films in which a study of aberration takes on the quality of high art: *Belle de Jour* (1967) and *Tristana* (1970). Even her more mature years did not stop that happening, as with

Opposite: Jane Fonda in strip-cartoon mood as the sexually-fantastic heroine of Barbarella (*Dino de Laurentiis, 1967*).

Left: The serene beauty of Catherine Deneuve – a face that launched a thousand kinks in such movies as Belle De Jour (*Five Film, 1967*).

Right: Monica Vitti as she was seen in any number of the films she made for Antonioni.

Opposite: Julie Christie and Terence Stamp in Far From The Madding Crowd *(Vic/Appia, 1967).*

The Hunger (1983) in which she was seen as a 1,000-year-old female vampire capable of both greedy sex and blood-sucking. However male film-makers regarded her, she is always and entirely her own woman – a liberated woman. Catherine Deneuve is the younger sister of film-star Françoise Dorleac who was, for a time, a star of some repute. But these things come and go. Star quality of the kind we are discussing is sustained by and nourishes itself.

The British woman star, Julie Christie, was for a time – again of the Swung Sixties – a luminary to observe with such movies as *Billy Liar* (1963) and *Darling* (1965) – both of them for director John Schlesinger, and both of them displaying her fine-boned beauty via a talent which represented the freer woman that was the mark of that time.

There was about Julie Christie the same air of sexual emancipation as there was about the Italian actress, Monica Vitti, who worked mainly with the great director Michelangelo Antonioni, perhaps acceding to his edict that: 'The film actor ought not to *understand*, he or she ought to be. One might argue that in order to be, he needs to understand. This is not true. If it were true the most intelligent actor would be the best actor. It is not possible to have true collaboration between actor and director. They work on two quite different levels.'

So was and is Vitti a dumb blonde? Certainly she has made some of her finest films with the director who held to that philosophy of cinema, from *L'Avventura* (1960) through *La Notte* (1961) and *The Eclipse* (1962) to *The Red Desert* (1964). Perhaps she, like Julie Christie, with Schlesinger, was too preoccupied with one director. But as a cinematic vision she has to a certain extent – like Christie – faded from view, only to be glimpsed occasionally in movies that she chooses specifically for herself.

Lollobrigida and Loren

There was, in the Sixties and Seventies, an influx of Italian actresses to the pantheon of goddesses. Vitti was one. And, of course, there was always Gina Lollobrigida, creamily beautiful, however coffee-black her hair; a true sex-symbol although her appeal was not sufficiently scaffolded by dramatic talent to stay the course.

For a time she went to Hollywood where she made such forgettable epics as *Solomon and Sheba* (1959) or *Go Naked In The World* (1961) or – even more forgettable – *Come September* (1961). She seemed to be in direct line of descent from the fiery-talented Anna Magnani, but seems now to have been much more diluted a proposition. She had a line in conniving bitchery which was never really given full expression until *King, Queen, Knave* (1972) for the Polish film director Jerzy Skolimowski, when she betrayed, with reticent sadism, David Niven (in one of the best rôles of his career).

More fulfilling as an actress, revealing herself with a purity and truth which still pulls the heart into its emotional orbit, is Sophia Loren, about whom Stanley Kaufman wrote in 'The New Republic': 'What is Sophia, who is she? She is sunlight, she is hearty warmth, she is great contentment with simple things; she is song and laughter, dance. She is a free-hearted lover, yet never depraved. The wonder is that, though she could not possibly exist, there she is: existing. She is not fake.'

As a love-song it may not rhyme, but it has its moments – and most men would agree with the sentiments that it contains so vividly beneath the sub-text of words. And hers is a career to wonder at, so near is it to the Cinderella-truth of a fairy story. A poverty-filled childhood, with *pasta* only to fill out those later-to-be-ample curves, she

Opposite: Gina Lollobrigida as a playgirl dress-designer opposite Rock Hudson in Come September – *when the leaves start to fall? (7 Pictures Corporation/ Raoul Walsh Enterprises, 1961).*

Left: Sophia Loren as The Millionairess *in which she starred with Peter Sellers (Dimitri de Grunwald, 1960).*

came from the people and it is they who cared for and caressed her reputation when it was in danger of shredding because of the Church-unblessed marriage of hers to producer Carlo Ponti.

She was a child of wartime. 'I think we would have starved to death if it hadn't been for the American G.I.'s – and their food parcels.' Her own liberation seemed to come with the liberation of her own country from Fascism, but it was her budding beauty which freed her from poverty. She became a 'star' of a kind in romantic strip-cartoons which used photographs to depict some impossibly melodramatic emotional circumstance.

From there, to the Rome studios, which were bursting into a life of feverish activity, with Carlo Ponti to guide her through the jungle of yes-men and contract signers.... Her first film was *Aida* (1953), with a voice dubbed by Renata Tebaldi and some plaudits from the critics. For instance, Bosley Crowther of the 'New York Times': '...the advantage is that a fine voice is set to a stunning form and face which is most grati-

fying (and unusual) in the operatic realm'.

The director who appreciated her best of all was Vittorio de Sica for whom she made the astonishing *Two Women* (1961). It was astonishing because it revealed an intensity of emotion which the very fact of her being a pin-up beauty had so far not revealed. Its story is of a mother and daughter, refugees, who encounter soldiers who rape the daughter. The anguish of the movie is still one of poignancy and despair.

It made up for the intriguing but superficially glamorous movies, such as *The Millionairess* (1960), in which she starred with Peter Sellers. De Sica once told me: 'I knew Sophia could do this kind of film, *Two Women*. She had lived that life of frustration and despair when she was young. She once told me about a friend of hers, when she was very young, who was raped by a soldier. It affected her very deeply. I think she was able to communicate that emotion on screen.'

Certainly the critics were unanimous in praise. Wrote Alexander Walker in the London 'Evening Standard': 'At the climax her motions are scored for brass and she plays them in a way that makes all her past films sound like interludes for seductive flutes.'

Her career, thereafter, seemed to alternate between such trifles as Chaplin's *A Countess From Hong Kong* (1966) to the more intense *Sunflower* (1969). It could afford the fluctuations, because Sophia Loren was established so completely in the public mind that it seemed she could do no wrong. She could even get away with something as awesomely awful as *The Priest's Wife* (1970). Sophia was and is Sophia.

Sophia, so good. But in which direction were cinema goddesses travelling? She combined a lacy femininity with a liberated mind, but, in fact, there was another genre of women stars to come forward. I once met Sophia Loren and asked her what was happening to women film stars? Who did she think would be the next idol? Presuming, of course, that she would still be within *her* slot in the pantheon.... 'Oh,' she said, 'But they are so young. It is almost perverse....' This was, in its way, true enough. The gymslip and ankle-sock brigade did, indeed, seem to be taking over.

But before understanding the Lolita-aspirants in the last chapter, let us consider those who never quite made it as deities.

Below: Sophia and Eleonora Brown as mother and daughter in Vittorio de Sica's fine movie La Ciociara (Two Women. *Champion/Marceau/ Cocinor/SGC, 1960).*

The Glimpsed Goddess

Sex appeal might well be considered the primary tool with which screen goddesses manipulate their audiences and their own personalities' effect upon their worshippers. But it is a tool with a very fine cutting edge; if it is blunted by a too-blatant representation then it becomes virtually a two-edged blade which can lacerate the wielder. Mae West might well be the exception that proves such a rule, but her ostentation was always wisely and shrewdly judged and mixed with a fair modicum of self-mockery which leavened the doughiness that such obviousness can cause.

The ill-fated Belinda Lee, for instance, was aware that the display of sex, of being a sex symbol, was – without any other qualities to amplify and help it along – a road to nowhere paved with all kind of good intentions: display without decorum.

I met her while she was under contract to the British Rank Organization in the 1950s, her strikingly blonde good looks shining out of such small toshes as *The Runaway Bus* (1953), *The Belles of St. Trinians* and *Murder By Proxy* (1954), *The Feminine Touch* and *Eyewitness* (1956) and *Nor The Moon By Night* (1958). She had a natural

Belinda Lee and George Baker in The Feminine Touch, *a drama about nursing (Ealing, 1956). Belinda's beauty overwhelmed her dramatic roles.*

sweetness of nature that did not seem to know how her looks could affect men – and, as a coming prospect, her audiences. She was married to Cornel Lucas, the much-liked stillsman at Pinewood Studios, Rank's home-base, who specialized in glamour photography and who could turn a wrinkled prune, by dint of his wonderous lighting, into a most seductively plumped grape. With Belinda he had no problems at all; she had the good complexion and the fine-honed looks of an English rose grown in middle-class soil in Budleigh Salterton.

She grumbled, I remember, about the way the Rank Organization was treating her. 'They don't know anything about stars. If they had Garbo under contract they'd just put her in a B-picture and hope she'd make it somehow. Certainly, they'd never put her name above the title of whatever movie she would be in.' This might give a wrong impression of her; she wasn't a grumbler by nature. It was just that she felt 'one of a crowd', one of the Rank so-called Charm School. And she was destined, seemingly, for high things. A very

147

senior Rank executive, I recall, told me she was the brightest light among the women starlets; a would-be jewel in the Rank crown.

There was an innocence about her that somehow made what happened inevitable – and tragic. She fell in love with a member of the Italian aristocracy and threw up husband, the Rank Organization, and her British career. She went to Italy to live and her blonde beauty attracted movies to her as though she were a magnet – mostly the wrong sort of movies. She was Lucretia Borgia in *The Nights of Lucretia Borgia* (1959) and other films included *The Story Of Joseph And His Brethren* (1960) and *Constantine And The Cross* (1961).

I met her again about this time and she was now more hardened with experience, her eyes slightly glazed with what one can only suppose was good living. 'That's all people see me as in the movies I make now,' she said. 'Sex. I'm just an object to them all. There's no subtlety about it. You might not see the versions of some of my films in England, but they're around . . . – the ones in which I'm topless, revealing all. If I'm not careful I'll end up in the hard-porn stuff: I've already been offered a couple and turned them down. But a girl's got to live and once you're typecast as I am, then it's hard to get out of the mould you've set in.'

She sounded bitter and, perhaps, she had cause to be. Anyway that bitterness, the implicit pain, was soon to come to an end. She was killed in a car crash in Italy in 1961. She was 26 years old.

She had seemed so astonishingly good looking that it was well nigh impossible to consider that she was no longer on earth in that so deliciously solid flesh. No, I don't suppose she had been a particularly bright girl but what she had she had known how to flaunt in a ladylike, seductive way. I remembered that she had said: 'I don't suppose I'm going to learn all that much about acting with the Rank Organization, but I am going to learn about being a personality . . . .' It had seemed naïve the way she said it; after all you can't *learn* an instinct, but I knew what she meant – and so did she.

'I'm not your outgoing sex-pot like Diana Dors, but I know that men like to look at me – and women, too. And that's important. You know, when I was in some Shakespeare play at school I was just in the background, but I knew – I was about four-teen – that *I* was the one who was being looked at, I knew that feeling of having the limelight of people's attention upon you. It was a very nice, warm feeling. It made me feel so wanted.'

The trouble is that for Belinda she wanted too many things for herself. There has to be, I suppose, a quality of Narcissus in all goddesses – indeed, in all actors and actresses. But that moment when the Narcissus-gaze becomes transfixed is the danger-moment, the time to drag one's glance away before the look itself locks one into a rigid stance with the looking-glass from which it is too difficult to recover.

So, for Belinda, the regrets are for what might have been . . . .

And she reminded me, too, of another blonde actress of around this time: Carole Lesley, who at one time liked to be known as Leslie Carroll. I met her on location in the Libyan desert while shooting *Ice Cold In Alex*. It was to have been her big moment; it turned out to be her big disaster. I just hope she recovered from it as, although I heard of her once or twice after that, she never swam again into the mainstream of cinema.

I think she had appeared in another film for J. Lee-Thompson, who was the director of *Ice Cold In Alex*. Anyway, he and the producer Kenneth Harper had seen some potential in the blonde girl from London. It was a potential that disappeared like the smell of water on the desert air.

The story concerns an ambulance during the North African campaign, carrying assorted types – John Mills and Anthony Quayle among them – to a hoped-for safety. Carole was one of the nurses aboard. It was a notably dangerous and grimy location in that one man died of being bitten by a scorpion and I was taken off in that same ambulance by a disease that brought me as close to that Great Cinema In The Sky as I would have cared to go at that time.

But before all that it really seemed that Carole just didn't know how to project her lines. Time after time she got it wrong and there comes a point when even the most equable director says that enough is enough. You have to be quite some star to persist in blowing lines that even the clapper-boy could get right.

For some reason it was thought that Carole liked me best of all the crew. Would I take her away and explain that she was

Diana Dors – a blonde bombshell determined to play Hollywood at its own game.

being replaced? I did that during a night-long movie show at the local movie house. It was an experience I do not want to have to repeat. Because, in opening the wound of her non-acceptance, a whole lot of unhappiness flooded out and it gave me some insight into what made this sort of girl want to become a goddess in the first place. It was the stuff about her father first, and then her stepfather . . . her nude modelling . . . the record producer she had lived with who had turned her out . . .

I wondered how she had survived it all. But she had. 'I thought if Diana Dors can do it, then so can I . . . after all she can't act. And I'm just as sexy as she is, even if I am less busty . . .'

A gutsy girl, Carole Lesley, and I'm sure she went on to better things. But not within the parameter of cinema, that's for sure. It wasn't that she wanted fame too much, it was that she needed fame *too* much – and there is a difference. Playwright John Osborne once wrote scathingly about those who want to *be* something, rather than *do* something. Goddesses may not be able to tell the two qualities apart – but it's there, it's there . . .

Diana Dors

It is intriguing that both these glamorous women should have mentioned Diana Dors as being, in some way, an aspect of the film-star life to which to aspire. For, as this chapter is an understanding of the goddesses who never quite made it, so Diana Dors herself never quite had it, either; although, for some she might well be seen to have reached the parthenon of pulchritude which she always ambitiously, sometimes awesomely, craved. The historian Ephraim Katz wrote, quite rightly, that 'the public remained largely apathetic toward her frank, exaggerated sexuality'. Until her death in her mid-fifties she could be seen – and obviously saw no harm in thus displaying herself – as a kind of institutionalized Big Momma, her other aspirations doubtless having been shelved upon that high-jutting bust which was always a most formidable feature of her screen personality.

She was actually born Diana Fluck in 1931 in Swindon, England and, during the course of long and hard-working early years as an entertainer, she eventually – as did most young girls of the time – ended up

Diana Dors looking for the glamorous life with Derek Farr in The Shop At Sly Corner (*US title:* Code Of Scotland Yard. *Pennant, 1946*).

Above: Diana Dors as the good-hearted gal with the good-hearted wrestler Joe Robinson. All very good-hearted in A Kid For Two Farthings *(London Films, 1955).*

Opposite: Dors in a different mood as the condemned murderess in Yield To The Night *(US title:* Blonde Sinner. *ABP, 1956).*

with the Rank Organization. She was not one, though, to be groomed like one of their were-sheep; besides, at that time, she had a husband, Dennis Hamilton, who was insistent in involving his wife in all kinds of publicity japes so that her name might be prominently displayed in the newspapers. I was there at the Venice Film Festival when she fell – bikini clad – into the lagoon from a gondola. No, of course, it was not manipulated or anything other than an accident . . . yet it so happened that a remarkable number of photographers were around to record the non-event and, somehow or other – such are the ways of picture editors – make it into an event that deserved recording in print.

Her career on screen was nearly as haphazard in the way she chose scripts and rôles – or had them chosen for her. Her first movie was *The Shop At Sly Corner* (1946) and then followed a rôle which seemed made for her in *Good Time Girl* (1948). She

seemed very much a representation of that seeming-freedom from wartime restriction which was swinging then as loose as her platinum blonde hair. She was, in fact, later to be touted as a rival to Marilyn Monroe, but what she lacked in that definition was any sense of vulnerability – which goddesses in that genre have to communicate. In *A Kid For Two Farthings* (1955) – Carol Reed's romantic evocation of London's East End – she was a working-girl who actually managed to convince one that she worked, as well as managing to look brassy and blatant. And in *Yield To The Night* (1956) she was given her chance at real drama by the director J. Lee-Thompson.

It was a curious, not to say outrageous bit of casting, the rôle of a convicted murderess awaiting execution, but Thompson always defended it by saying that he recognized in her acting qualities which had always been underneath that all too obvious exterior (presumably in the same way that a

woman's real face can be obscured by layers of make-up). The movie was based on a story by Thompson's then wife, Joan Henry, and required a subtlety of interpretation to be apparent beneath the overt sexuality of the woman who was, ostensibly, based on the real-life Ruth Ellis, hanged for the murder of her lover. It was Diana Dors' real chance at the drama that she once told me meant everything to her. It was a chance that was muffed. It may well have been the context of screenplay and direction, but the idea seemed no more real than cut-out charades. Strangely, it seemed as though the story were in so much bad taste – and yet it was a story that should have rent the heart with its ironic pity and compassion.

All goddesses of the Dors' kind make their way to Hollywood and, sure enough, that is just what Diana Dors did, making one or two films which insisted on typecasting her as the kind of woman-who-did-him-wrong. Rod Steiger, who worked with her, remembered that 'she had a tremendous vitality, but no technique or real acting experience at all. She was very much a personality – or that is how she saw herself, anyway. She was difficult to play to, because of that. It was not that she could not remember her lines – she was too professional for that – but she was too *aware* of how she was saying them. She rolled along on top of the lines, instead of working *through* them. Somebody had obviously once told her that she was a sex symbol – and she had believed it.'

Certainly the whole of the British press had been telling her and their readers just that for years, so that it was hardly her fault that she had begun to believe them. But, in reality, her extroversion of sexuality was too obvious to be anything other than off-putting; and that is just not the sort of quality that one associates with real sex symbols.

She once told me: 'I don't think much of my looks, but it's the overall impression that the public receives, don't you think? If you tell them that something is attractive, they end up by thinking it *is* attractive.' In other words: you can fool the people all of the time . . . . The public, however, were not that easily fooled. In later years she made some horror movies and, in her middle age proved that she could act. But the public had never really regarded her as

a sex symbol, even if the press had. She was pigeon-holed, consciously or subconsciously, as one of those species of people that British people love to contemplate while not particularly envying their life style: the eccentrics.

Bo Derek

From eccentric . . . to concentric, having the same centre of ambition and desire to become a goddess of the screen. And as a prime, pulchritudinous example of that let us think upon Bo Derek, a girl-woman in whom Nature has conspired to ensure that, like an egg, she is all curves – and most of them assembled in the altogether right place. The critic Steven H. Scheuer described her as 'one of the most ravishingly beautiful women who ever stepped in front of a movie camera', mainly on the strength of her film *10* (1979). In this she played the indiscreet object of desire for Dudley Moore who, as a middle-aged songwriter of failing sexuality, pursues her in the hope of gaining her – and regaining his powers.

The figure of the title comes from the sexual rating which he imposes on the women whom he stalks and Miss Derek is rated 10, the highest that could be achieved. A film flawed of its kind, it nevertheless had some pertinent comments to make about the male-female relationship. And the reality of the Derek character actually taking Dudley Moore to bed awakens in him – and presumably in the male members of the audience – the awesome realization that the hunted can become the hunter, that women have desires as well as men.

That seduction – of the man by the woman – was accomplished to the sound of Ravel's Bolero, which gave it a brief spell of audio fame before it was then taken by British ice-skating champions Torvill and Dean. The precise and fastidious Maurice Ravel might well have been amused at the use to which his composition was being put. It was a film to make any woman a star – especially a woman as beautiful as Bo Derek. But, how to follow it up?

Miss Derek is married to former actor John Derek, another extraordinarily handsome creature who set out to manage and, presumably market, his desirable wife, so her films afterwards were scheduled to

157

Some lucky chimp and Bo Derek in Tarzan The Ape Man *(MGM, 1981).*

zan saga since Elmo Lincoln first swung from the lianas in 1918, this is the only version that gives precedence to the "civilized" woman, Jane, over the ape-man, leaving the eponymous hero not only speechless but essentially an onlooker to the main action. It is a shift of dramatic emphasis that in no way represents a feminist re-reading of the legend.

'On the contrary, the only apparent rationale of John Derek's resolutely sexist treatment of the old yarn is a besotted desire to celebrate his wife's physical attributes in various exotic settings and erotic costumes.'

The review hammered home the fact that the whole thing was a 'multi-million dollar lingerie commercial'. Miss Derek's undergarments may have meant something in *10* but here they were just so much grubby underwear ... or, at least, that was the opinion of many critics who saw the film which seemed to get a very limited release in Britain and, indeed, throughout the world.

Other films – usually engineered by Bo Derek – came and went, but the beauty of Bo never quite coincided as spectacularly with the beast of the box-office as it had done in *10*.

One of the reasons for this may well have been that the public doesn't mind its goddesses being blatant in the projection of sexuality, and all those feminine attributes which distinguish women from men – but, instinctively, there is a resentment about and resistance against a *knowing* blatancy, a wink-and-nudge realization that I'm manipulating you ... and you're simple enough to accept it.

Pia Zadora

The cynic might well enough have said that nobody ever lost money under-estimating the intelligence of the public but there is an unconscious knowledge among the public when it knows that it is being got at: it is then that it revolts against the publicity that is being foisted upon it to make it accept, a time when it runs untrue to hype.

This occurred, too, with Pia Zadora, a curvaceous bundle of sex appeal with a millionaire husband who was obviously prepared to give his young wife everything she wanted to become a film star – a film, even. Her first and most memorable movie was *Butterfly* (1981), a treatment which had

display her charms in the most interesting and provocative way. One such was *Tarzan The Ape Man* (1981) which Mr Derek himself directed. This was a somewhat bizarre re-working of the Edgar Rice Burroughs story with Tarzan (Miles O'Keeffe) playing a somewhat subdued second fiddle to Jane (Bo Derek), daughter of Victorian explorer (Richard Harris) who is always on the verge of losing her honour and can only retain same by being rescued by the ape-man with whom, at the last, she decides to spend her days in the jungle.

The British Film Institute's 'Monthly Film Bulletin' said of it: 'Of all the screen adaptations of Edgar Rice Burroughs' Tar-

spread its wings from an original novel by James M. Cain, with the action transferred to a disused silver mine in the Nevada desert. Here works caretaker Stacy Keach, alone with his memories, a reverie soon to be lewdly interrupted by the arrival of Ms Zadora who informs him that she is his daughter. She makes so many passes, then, at the poor bewildered chap that it is no wonder that she mesmerizes him into making love to her. This is the kind of unlawful relationship which soon lands them in court. Human incest stories are not considered entirely appropriate to the society in which we live.

The trouble here was, as I have said before, not just the blatancy – but the knowing blatancy. Ms Zadora's attributes certainly hung well but the balance was overturned by the way in which all the sexuality was thrust at an audience, without any humour at all, for instance when she takes a ladle of milk straight from a cow's teat and husks suggestively: 'I like it warm, with froth on top.' As a come-on this was about as subtle as a street accident – and a lot less convincing in its impact. The 'Film Year Book for 1983' referred to the film as 'comically overwrought' and commented on the 'abundance of posture-striking, supplemented by numerous variations on a pout'.

Ms Zadora might well have felt herself to be a very lonely lady, a fact which may well have inspired another of her films, *The Lonely Lady* (1982) from a novel by the sexily best-selling writer Harold Robbins. The story of *The Lonely Lady* is about the trials and misfortunes of a Hollywood screenwriter, Jerilee Randall (Ms Zadora) who has to sleep her way to the top of her profession, a journey including various methods of sex from ordinary sex to lesbianism and includes an early scene of sexual assault with the nozzle of a hose-pipe.

The BFI's 'Monthly Film Bulletin' stated: 'It's the solemnity of this misconceived concoction that most appals. Slogging grimly through the pathetic apology for a plot ... Pia Zadora has mercifully abandoned the baby doll pout she sported throughout *Butterfly*, but found no noticeable expression to replace it. Her stolidity keeps good company, since a less personable cast can rarely have been assembled even for a poverty-row quickie.'

The loneliness, in fact, of the long-distance bummer. Ms Zadora, though, may not have been amused by all these attacks – and jokey references to herself in Hollywood by other stars – but, meeting her, she refused to let such jibes get her down. She knows where she is going and her enthusiasm for her objective in being a goddess is something she can express with a fervour and intelligence which comes in pleasant contrast to the kind of movies in which she has found herself (or, rather, not found herself, to be more precise).

She told me: 'I know I have a good body and I know the public enjoys looking at me. What's wrong with that? Sure I've made mistakes, but then who doesn't? Marilyn Monroe made an awful lot of mistakes, but they're forgotten now. It's the legend that remains; that's all that counts.

'I suppose you could say that I was determined. Well, I am determined. I'm lucky to be in a position to be able to choose movies that I want to be in and if I choose wrongly, well, I hope that I can make mistakes and build on them. That what it's all about after all. You've got to keep going; you've got to ride over all the criticisms, although I agree you have to learn from those criticisms – and, hopefully, build on them.'

If a fraction of her personal communication to me could be transferred to film, then I think Pia Zadora would be well on her way to becoming one of the contemporary goddesses of the screen. But the films she has made so far don't augur all that well for the future.

Collins, Kristel and Lange

The future for Joan Collins might well now seem well behind her at the age of 51, having been born in London on 23 May 1933. But it is as though age has whipped her into an even stronger frenzy of flaunting – which, admittedly, is quite considerable. The trouble is that it has never been completely accepted or accommodated by the public, so that although her name means something it does not ultimately pass the acid test of being a goddess – where the surname is sufficient information to impart to others just who is being talked about. Garbo, Bardot, Monroe .... Collins might just as easily be the drink John Collins. Her recent appearances in the soap-series, 'Dynasty', has given her a certain appeal, but then most of the films in which she was

involved have been soap-operas of one kind or another: usually sexual. Her sister, Jackie Collins, is a novelist of the Harold Robbins variety – if not as mass-appealing – and both of them have persisted in projecting sex as the staple ingredient of what might be considered their personalities.

Joan Collins began with reasonably interesting British productions such as *I Believe In You* (1952), but her involvement in Hollywood brought out the sexiness in her and such films as *The Girl In The Red Velvet Swing* (1955) seemed to predominate.

Then, in recent years, Joan Collins, as though to assure everyone her sex appeal had not diminished with the advancing years – that she could, indeed, advance through them – made a series of films in which she also had an interest in terms of the production. The first of these was *The Stud* (1978), which was about a randy young man who managed to cut a sexual swathe through any number of women, and then *The Bitch* (1979), which had Ms Collins herself a similarly potent member of the opposite gender. These films were distinguished, if that is the word, by lovemaking in bizarre situations, such as a lift – sexual elevation in an elevator, in fact. Whether or not Ms Collins had any financial interest in *Nutcracker* (1982) – a title whose pun was not without admirers astonished at its tastelessness – certainly she was rampantly in it, as what amounted to a madame of a kind. 'Unremittingly witless' was the least of the criticisms of a story which was about a Russian ballet-dancer (Finola Hughes) who becomes involved with a Western dancing school, the morals of whose members are certainly no better than they ought to be – or, indeed, are.

And there, so far as cinema goes, the matter rests for Joan Collins, who seems to have found a safe niche for her beauty in TV

Joan Collins being chastized by anxious mum (Hermione Baddeley) in Cosh Boy (*Daniel Angel Films, 1953*).

Collins goes Hollywood – for The Girl In The Red Velvet Swing *(TCF, 1955).*

soap-opera. An extremely attractive woman, of an elegant contour and appearance, she has, however, one aspect which seems to have been lacking in all her appearances on film. She lacks, despite her physical appearance to the contrary, style – a very necessary ingredient or compound in what makes the sexual chemistry that leads to the kind of goddess quality we are talking about.

This quality is similarly lacking in another actress who has been one of the most exposed – in all senses of that word – in recent years. Sylvia Kristel's forte was

the soft-porn movie which aspired to commercial success, and with such films as *Emmanuelle* (1974) that kind of success was certainly there. This, directed by a film-maker with the unlikely name of Just Jaeckin, concerned the erotic adventures of a young woman in the Far East (again, bizarre locations are somehow supposed to heighten our interest in the proceedings).

Born in Holland Ms Kristel had, in fact, begun her exhibitionist life as a mannequin and her slim build might not seem at all suited to the nudity that was demanded of her in the films that were her professional

163

context for so long. She appeared in *Emmanuelle II* (1975) and her name became synonymous with a certain kind of free-living movie which purported to be about a certain kind of free loving.

In conversation she was as frank as her movies, admitting that 'my breasts are small but they do seem larger when they are seen in films. Also my success is because I can make quite an erotic panting noise, so that it sounds as though I am reaching orgasm. In fact, of course, one often has to dub that noise on after the film has been shot. So it is rather funny; here am I making all those sexy noises while a sound recordist is looking on, doubtless wondering whether he can get away in time to have a good luncheon.'

But, although a lot of Ms Kristel was seen by an international public – at one time *Emmanuelle* reached the top of the box-office ratings in America – she is not of goddess-calibre. One can see why, for instance, when she appeared in a mainstream film, *Airport '79 Concorde* (1979), which revealed that she could make little impact as an actress engaged in the ordinary day-to-day business of conversation and emotion. There was, it could be seen, no more to her than met the eye.

But, at the opposite side of that professional track, can be seen an actress, such as Jessica Lange, whose outstanding dramatic abilities seem, paradoxically, to be in inverse proportion to the star quality that is beamed at an audience. Despite all her yeoman-conquest of her often punishing rôles, as in *The Postman Always Rings Twice* (1981), she is not one who can illuminate an audience's collective heart in the way that actresses who are inferior can do without her skill and emotional commitment.

William Sylvester, Collins and Finola Hughes in Nutcracker *(Rank, 1982).*

She began with a kind of disadvantage, anyway, being cast opposite the biggest scene-stealer in the movies: a giant ape called Kong in the 1976 remake of *King Kong*, by producer Dino de Laurentiis.

Although well enough made – by director John Guillermin – this reworking of the great, legendary film could never hope to match the original, which derived as much of its strength from its folkloric quality as its movie-making skills. Although more humorously overt in its realization of the lust that Kong feels for the white girl it adores, the original said more about primitive desire, though showing less. It was, predictably enough, savaged by critics who felt it was a case very much of *lèse-majesté*. At a later press conference Ms Lange admitted that the film hadn't been the success that she, and everyone concerned, had hoped it would be. 'But it did get me into movies,' she told me. 'And we all have to start somewhere.' She had been a model in New York after dancing with the Opéra-Comique in Paris and her movements had an eloquence which spoke what

The ever-pouting, rather attractive Sylvia Kristel.

Above: Jessica Lange and Roy Scheider in one of the few quiet times of All That Jazz (Robert Alan Aurthur, Daniel Melnick, 1979).

Right: Kristel and a lover in Emmanuelle (Orphée, 1974).

might be presumed to be the language of a goddess, a Parnassian vocabulary of suppressed desire.

In Bob Fosse's *All That Jazz* (1979) she was the glimpsed goddess of wished-for death that the choreographer Roy Scheider obviously craves for through his obsessed and obsessing life. It was not so much a role as an elaboration of a showcase which showed her blonde beauty to real advantage, an advantage which was very much lost in her next and most famous film,

Frances (1982). This was an adaptation of an autobiography by Frances Farmer, who achieved some small reputation in the 1930s as a film actress but who ended up as an alcoholic and an inmate of a mental hospital. She was later released, after what amounted to a lobotomy, and her harrowing story was bound to set goose-pimples squawking as a piece of spiritual and mental grand guignol.

Ms Lange as Ms Farmer was quite remarkable, going all the way through all

This thing is bigger than all of us – Jessica Lange in the special-effects grip of Kong in the remake of King Kong (Dino de Laurentiis, 1976).

One of Jessica Lange's better roles – as the deranged film actress of the Thirties, Frances Farmer, in Frances *(EMI/Brooks Films, 1982).*

the circles of a Dante-esque Hell with awesome deliberation and power. The trouble with the performance was, as most critics noted, that it was too on the top: one could sense, if not see, the cogs working. A great artist may go to all kinds of trouble to gain his effects but the result has to seem spontaneous if it is to spark with the public. The effect of Ms Lange's performance was not at all spontaneous; to judge it at its most extreme it was mechanical.

Audrey Hepburn

In pursuing the ultimate ideal of goddess, those who take up the hunt realize – sometimes too late – that the ultimate has changed its shape and its format in mid-chase: in terms of Lewis Carroll – the Snark has become a Boojum. Ironically, too often it seems that the more one chases and hounds the object of ambition the more elusive it becomes. In consideration of these lights that failed, let us consider as a contrast a girl who succeeded – almost without meaning to: Audrey Hepburn.

Born in 1929 of Irish-Dutch parents in Belgium she had a face whose wide, as-tonishingly impressive eyes were her main feature – and that face assured her much modelling work in Britain for such personal items as cosmetics. She was very much of the 1948–51 time when a svelte slimness was in and swan-like necks such as hers were not so much out as elegantly angled away from her body. She was, in her way, a spirit of the woods, and it is surprising that nobody ever asked her to star in J.M. Barrie's 'Mary Rose' which would have been amazingly apt for her kind of beauty. She began in a small way with such films as *Laughter In Paradise* (1951) and then *The Lavender Hill Mob* (1951) and followed that with *Secret People* (1952) as a young ballet dancer. It was not, despite its credentials and its director (Thorold Dickinson) a very distinguished movie, but her looks brought her to the attention of Hollywood and she won an Oscar next year for her part as the princess in William Wyler's *Roman Holiday* (1953).

It seemed appropriate for her Ondine-similar beauty that *Roman Holiday* should have been a kind of modern fairy-tale with newspaperman Gregory Peck falling in love

Eddie Albert, Audrey Hepburn and Gregory Peck in the royal fairy-tale, Roman Holiday *(Paramount, 1953).*

169

Vows a-tremble, novice Audrey Hepburn ministers to Peter Finch in The Nun's Story *(Warner, 1959).*

Opposite: Audrey Hepburn as she was with Albert Finney in Two For The Road *(TCF, 1966).*

with her princess without realizing – at first – that she is of the blood royal. A ridiculous conception? Of course, but handled with delicacy and not a little wit and very much suited to the times in which it appeared.

This settled Audrey Hepburn – born, interestingly enough, Edda Hepburn van Heemstra – into the mould of fey, wayward beauty which a string of movies, such as *Sabrina Fair* (1954), and even her role as Natasha in *War and Peace* (1956), did not break: she was lustrous and she was mysterious. Billy Wilder's *Love In The Afternoon* (1957) extended that aura just a little, but not all that much. 'I so often felt,' she once told me, 'that my film career was simply an expansion of my modelling career. I was a walking clothes-horse again . . . .'

That she could act was proved dramatically in such movies as *The Loudest Whisper*

(1962) or *The Nun's Story* (1959), wherein she bared the innermost soul of a religious novice who 'has doubts' and eventually leaves the order to which she had felt herself so crushingly called. One of her most interesting films was, in fact, *Wait Until Dark* (1967) in which she played a blind girl at the mercy of a creepy villain, Alan Arkin, and only able to fight him when she extinguishes all the lights in the house so that she and he are on equal terms of darkness.

So, a goddess-attainment of a kind. Yet it had always seemed that success had pursued *her* rather, as is so often the case, the other way around. It was how she explained it herself to me. 'I suppose like any girl at an impressionable early age one longs for fame in movies, but it never really occurred to me that it would happen and when it did I didn't really understand why it had hap-

Classic style – Cary Grant and Katharine Hepburn in Howard Hawks' Bringing Up Baby (RKO, 1938).

pened. I didn't know how to engineer that success; it engineered me.

'I think it was because I was the face for the time; my kind of gamin looks were somehow or other suited exactly to what people wanted: what women wanted to look like and what men wanted women to look like. It had a good deal to do with the fashionable magazines of the time, too: 'Harper's Bazaar', 'Vogue' – all those that affect how the top women want to dress and look. I was of that specialization and that way of looking that people wanted at that particular time. I don't know how it would work today; I don't know how people want to look today. I think people don't know themselves; that's why there are so many female images around. And, don't forget, television has fragmented so many things. I think it has fragmented the way people want to look.'

Opposite: Classic stylist.

Katharine Hepburn

In conversation Audrey Hepburn paid fond tribute to her namesake, Katharine Hepburn – 'that marvellous face. It's all right talking about her bone-structure, but there's something so marvellously expressive that you feel it can say anything without saying a word.' And, here again is a woman who might be considered almost as an antique goddess who made it into the Parthenon almost without meaning to, backing into the limelight that she so scorns that she never participates in any of the junkets that publicity promotions demand of current-day actors and actresses.

She has, indeed, always treated the film industry with what might be termed disdain in her terms – arrogance in those who do not like her. She was at one time called 'box office poison', although let us pray that some other actress might succumb to that

Hepburn with Spencer Tracy in Adam's Rib, *one of many delightful duels they made (MGM, 1949).*

John Wayne predictably said that working with her 'was some treat; she sure is some lady', and Bogart had said 'she's a very patrician woman but that doesn't stop her being surprisingly earthy when she wants to be. She has my deepest respect.'

There are those in Hollywood who considered her to be so stand-offish that she 'wouldn't give you the time of day' (as one producer once told me). But there is under the surface of that resolute, thoroughbred exterior a sense of smoulder which I believe the public senses in spite of appearances. In 1982 she made *On Golden Pond* with Henry Fonda – a study in old age which was a most intelligent and discreet siphoning of tears. And there one could see the fact of her deification as complete and unspoiled by her age. She who had seemed above films was, as always, revealed to be a consummate film actress. It was some revelation.

She once told a rare interviewer: 'I suppose at first I wasn't all that keen on Hollywood – or, at any rate, the kind of image that Hollywood presented in the early 1930s, all brash glitter and money-mad moguls. But you get used to things. I got used to Hollywood and I guess Hollywood got used to me.'

So the pursuit for a kind of immortality cannot simply be seen as the unsinkable in pursuit of the unattainable. To those who have already shall be given and to those who have not, not? Certainly, as I have tried to prove in this chapter, those who go a-flaunting too obviously will never attain divine status, while there are those such as the Hepburns to whom shall be added more of the same – without even being asked.

So let us end this chapter with one of those who have chased the illusion of being a goddess and found that … it is an illusion. Betty Blythe was noted for the transparency of one single gown worn in *Queen of Sheba* (1921). At her screen test she was asked to choose one dress from the thirty-six gowns called for by the part. She later said 'I chose one with a great peacock. Later we had twenty-two of them on our ranch in the country. When you walked in this costume which had pearls to the knees, the legs would come out. When you stood still there was that glorious peacock right across the body. "Oh," I said, "the peacock – that's for me. That'll make the public remember me. That'll make me a star."'

The point is: who *was* Betty Blythe?

kind of wonderful lethality. Born in 1909 of rich parents she began her career in show-business via the theatre, and was noticeable enough on Broadway to make the journey into movies. She did not choose well at first – or, rather, films were not chosen well for her – and such journeyman movies as *Spitfire* (1934) and *The Little Minister* (1934) were the result. But she achieved better with *Alice Adams* (1935) and then *Sylvia Scarlett* (1935), in this last posing as a boy.

She was in screen terms very much a man's woman, able to match the blithe wit of Cary Grant in such comedies as *Bringing Up Baby* (1938) and then settling for the more rugged temperament of Spencer Tracy in a series of films for which they became famous, such as *Pat And Mike* (1952) and *Adam's Rib* (1949). She was able to cope with Humphrey Bogart in *The African Queen* (1952) and later with John Wayne in *Rooster Cogburn* (1975) which was a reprise of the character that Wayne had created in *True Grit*.

The Body...and the Voice

'A Sensual Child Comes Of Age' proclaimed the headline in 'Time' magazine. It was atop a feature article about some new young European beauty and that headline could be taken, at first glance, to mean just what it says. But, take it apart, and it also says something about our screen goddesses, all sensual children in themselves. For each of them comes from their own age – horses for courses, to put it vulgarly. That is why it is interesting to compare two of the cinema's greatest goddesses, even though their beauty and their talents may seem very disparate in the way the public reacts to them: Ava Gardner and July Garland.

They both came to the top at about the same time and both in their different ways presented to their audiences ideals which those audiences felt might well be attainable if they worshipped long enough. Ava Gardner had the body; Judy Garland the voice.

Ava Gardner once told me: 'I sometimes envy the young film actresses of today because they have so much more freedom than we had. If we offended somebody in power at a studio then that was it; you must never forget that Hollywood was, in essentials, a factory town. That we were in the business of glamour was beside the point; we might just as well have been making cosmetics.'

Certainly Ava Gardner, whose career we have already discussed, was and is one of the most glamorous of all those in the glamour business. And sparse though her appearances are these days, she remains a goddess. She arrived at that deific destination by the most remarkable of all routes: simply by *being*.

The restless spirit that was Judy Garland was never content with simply being; she had to get out there and fight to be somebody, even if there were few people to battle with. Most of all – as her tormented private life testified – she battled with herself. Her talent always remained, though, however much carnage was wrought upon that spiritual battlefield.

She was born Frances Gumm in Grand Rapids, Minnesota, of vaudeville parents, and with her sister she went on stage with the title of The Gumm Sisters. At the age of 13 she was contracted to MGM and made her screen debut in *Every Sunday* (1936). There followed many, many films in a gruelling schedule that traumatized the early part of her life and about which she was bitterly articulate in her later life: 'I never had any childhood. My school was the studio and that stood in as parent as well.' Her voice, if not her open face, was her fortune and she used it to wonderful sentimental effect in such films as *Babes On Broadway* (1941), *For Me And My Gal* (1942), *Girl Crazy* (1943), *Thousands Cheer* (1943), *Meet Me In St Louis* (1944), *The Clock* (1945), *The Pirate* (1947) and then the great *A Star Is Born* (1954), which was severely cut at the time but which can now be seen in a fairly full version.

There was in the Garland voice, as there was in the Garland life and legend, a vibrato of sentiment which, unless you knew her and her story, might seem to have been constructed from old showbusiness gossip about the show having to go on . . . but it was a vibrato that rang true despite all the ruinous decisions she made about drink and personal relationships. Her yearning power – so marvellously in evidence in all her movies – was for real. And people sense that instinctively.

For instinct is what moves people out towards their goddesses. Perhaps such

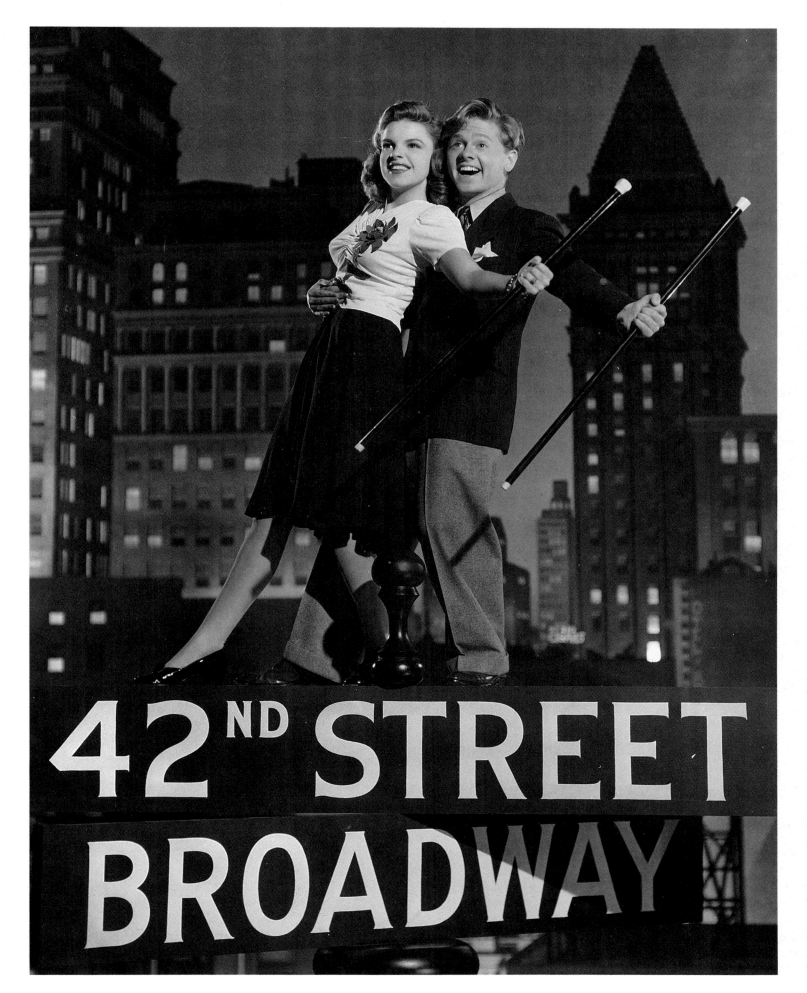

actresses start out – almost inevitably – with the spirit of Narcissus within them but the public recognizes that that spirit is one that they can share. The public becomes a mirror for the goddess and the goddess becomes a mirror for the public: through a glass mythically.

Gimmicks help, of course – but not much. Betty Grable once recalled that all the fuss about her 'million dollar legs' was caused by a new publicist at the Fox studios. 'When I was seventeen or eighteen the studio got a new publicity man who wanted to impress people. He decided to get something flashy and splashy going and just happened to choose me. It was all fixed. He told me, "We'll run competitions and say you have the best legs." So their phoney contest took place and I was given the cup. But once they'd taken the pictures the cup went back. Then they had my legs sculp-

tured, but all I wanted was that cup!'

There were other innovatory gimmicks: the sweaters filled so amply by Lana Turner and the Jennifer Jones shirts worn by her in *Duel In The Sun* (1946). Then the bras referred to as Les Lollos after Gina Lollobrigida's appearance in *Bread, Love And Dreams* (1953).

But these are exterior novelties that only work for a time, as an introduction to the personality that is being sold by the movie – to the image that is being presented for public delectation. Can these tremendous vessels of femininity survive the television age? It was put to me once that there could never be any real stars on TV itself because 'the viewer can always stand up and be bigger than what is being shown'. That which is worshipped, therefore, has to be all those many feet high: this thing is bigger than we are.

*Jamming with the best.
Judy in* A Star Is Born.

'Time' magazine has written: 'For more than a century the camera has conspired with artists and models to create successive ideals of allure. One early ideal was Parisian: gaunt and *haut monde*, with cheekbones so prominent you could cut your finger on them, if you dared touch them. Then, as the Hollywood cinema shouldered its way to eminence, the world standard became the active, approachably American woman, radiating health and common sense. Now there is another ideal, a new symmetry of features raising its profile in still and moving pictures. It holds all the history and mystery of an older world, all that intelligence and sophistication, but with one bright eye fixed on the dream of international stardom.'

So the goddess trail goes on into the future. Where are the Garbos of tomorrow? The Harlows? The Garlands? We shall see in the next chapter about the aspirant goddesses, the new acolytes in the temple of contemporary Venus.

Child-Women and the Goddesses of the Future

In the beginning was Shirley Temple . . . well not quite true because there had always been child stars. There was for instance a goddess of a different kind, although juvenile, in Judy Garland who with *The Wizard of Oz* (1939) put all our hearts through the wringer with the power and vulnerability of her magic. Then there was Margaret O'Brien who was to hold juvenile sway for a time, as in *Meet Me In St Louis* (1944). Such a technician was she that she was able to ask her director, Vincente Minnelli: 'When I cry do you want the tears to come all the way down my cheeks, or just a little way?'

But of these Lilliputian creatures Shirley Temple was the tot who danced and sang her way into the community heart of the world lisping about animal crackers in her soup and taking everyone on a magical voyage on the Good Ship Lollipop. She was driven onwards and upwards by one of those dominating stage-mothers who animate their own ambition with the power of their children's talent. After some early successes Shirley became the World's Sweetheart – a post recently held by Mary Pickford – and with such films as *Wee Willie Winkie, Heidi, Rebecca Of Sunnybrook Farm* (all 1938) she established a reputation that is untarnished, and sued to protect it after Graham Greene, the novelist, overstepped the mark in a review which was held to be libellous. The magazine which carried the review was bankrupted.

She made *Wee Willie Winkie* for John Ford and he said later, 'She was a great professional. There was nothing you could

Shirley Temple in Rebecca Of Sunnybrook Farm – *a long way after Mary Pickford – dancing with Bill Robinson (Mr. Bojangles). (TCF, 1938.)*

Shirley Temple had taken over where Mary Pickford had stopped – not only The Littlest Rebel *but* The Littlest Sweetheart *(TCF, 1935).*

teach her. She was spot on cue and knew her lines.' Seeing those films today one can see the remarkable expertise that went into them. It was not just that one had to make allowances for the fact that Shirley Temple was a child; her ability made her seem not to need that patronizing assumption. She was a star in her own right and throughout the Thirties she twinkled with a relentless energy that made her the despair of some of the adult stars who worked with her.

But, although Shirley Temple was a child star, you never thought of sex within the context of the circumstance she generated. That was to come later. Stanley Kubrick's version of the Nabokov novel, *Lolita* (1962) was a visualization of a notorious story about a man falling madly and deeply in love with an under-age girl. Sue Lyon

played the girl, while James Mason was the man, Humbert Humbert. It was a film that was – like the book – at once poignant and comic, flash and fanciful ... and deeply felt. Sue Lyon, herself, seemed to disappear from view immediately afterwards, but she seemed to be the forerunner of child-women who, within the context of their youth, generated a kind of sex appeal.

This reached a kind of apogee in 1976 with Martin Scorsese's *Taxi Driver* which had the young Jodie Foster as a child prostitute, whose pimp, the returned Vietnam veteran Robert De Niro kills in an orgy of slaughter. Her immediate remarks about 'How do you want to make it?' gave the film an advance reputation which was, in fact, erased by the brilliance and depth of the actual narrative itself.

Above: Sue Lyon sucks on a straw and James Mason bites on his lip in Lolita *(Seven Arts/AA/Anya/ Transworld, 1962).*

Overleaf: Tatum O'Neal and father Ryan in Paper Moon, *a father-and- daughter act of great appeal (Saticoy, 1973).*

Another child-woman of this period of the late 1970s was Tatum O'Neal, daughter of the film-star Ryan O'Neal with whom she appeared in *Paper Moon* (1973). She appeared in such films as *The Bad News Bears* (1976) with such old-time professionals as Walter Matthau, who later grumbled to me: 'She was a real scene-stealer. It's true what they say about children and animals as upstagers.' He was, though, to go on to make *Little Miss Marker* (1980) with an even smaller child, Sara Stimson. Perhaps it was to prove that it could be done!

All kinds of Krafft seemed to be Ebing out of the cupboard in the way of sexuality, as the word paedophilia was bandied about as though it were something that had only recently been invented. However, maturity was gradually coming in again, helped by the kind of film in which Tatum O'Neal starred with Richard Burton: *Circle Of Two* (1982) in which she is the teenage girl who falls into lust with a middle-aged artist. This film was so inordinately bad that it just had to do damage to the child-woman syndrome. It did.

Nastassia Kinski

So the goddesses of the future emerge, as Venus from the sea of the future. Sure enough, they look younger than the years of past deities, but they are still women, even though they may have been experienced when teenagers.

Such a one, for example, is Nastassia Kinski, daughter of the actor Klaus Kinski, and former girlfriend of Roman Polanski who cast her as *Tess* and photographed her beauty as though he were only now rediscovering it.

It is, perhaps, too early to tell yet about the quality of her work, although she has certainly put in a *lot* of work: from the awesome fetishism of *Cat People* (1983) – in which she turned into a panther to kill the man after making love – to Francis Ford Coppola's endearing *One From The Heart* (1982). *Cat People* was a remake of an original classic and *Unfaithfully Yours* (1984) is another reworking of an original cinematic touchstone. It is as though her classic beauty is relied upon for that which endures. Howard Zieff, the director of *Un-*

Jodie Foster, the reason for the slaughter that culminates Taxi Driver *(Italo-Judeo, 1976).*

faithfully Yours, said: 'She has great instinct. She still hasn't cracked the surface of all that beauty and talent.'

At the moment, though, she is decoration – a marvellous adornment. Jean-Jacques Beineix, who directed her in *The Moon In The Gutter* (1984), said about the role she plays: 'Nastassia was perfect for the part. I was completely seduced by her. I caressed her face on my editing table. But I found that she requires a lot of care, love and work. She makes great demands – and woe to the director who cannot satisfy them. You have to be strong with Nastassia. Otherwise she will devour you.'

It is the true goddess-trait – to devour her worshippers before they devour her. It is the ritualist in the holy grove that Sir James Frazer, in his great work of anthropology 'The Golden Bough', talks about, although a priest/god/king could just as easily be substituted.

'Time' magazine called Nastassia Kinski the 'New Marilyn' and it might well have meant that she also had her fair share of vulnerabilities about the way her life was being formed.

There are others around of the same sensuous beauty as Kinski. We can see it in Joanna Cassidy in *Under Fire* (1984) – although her tough elegance has yet to be proved – and certainly in Isabelle Adjani whose work with François Truffaut on such films as *The Story of Adèle H* (1975). She, too, is one who tries to work with the best directors, as she did with Polanski on *The Tenant* (1976) and then again with the German *Wunderkind*, Werner Herzog, on *Nosferatu*.

But, of them all, Kinski seems to be the one who will endure the longest – certainly on her present rate of progress. As 'Time' magazine wrote: 'Who loves you, baby? Who watches you and watches over you?

Nastassia Kinski in Roman Polanski's Tess, *based on Thomas Hardy's classic Wessex novel 'Tess of the D'Urbervilles' (Renn-Burrill, 1979).*

Face of the Future: Nastassia Kinski smiles for One From The Heart, *that title a neat enough comment on goddesses in general (Zoetrope Studios, 1982).*

Who protects and exposes you? Who finds poetry in every pore, grace in your limbs, mystery behind those eyes? Whose passive power turns you on, gets you acting and acting up, captures your gifts? Who can never forget you? Who is your perfect love, baby? The camera is.'

And, of course, it always was so. The camera at once breaks and makes the goddess. It is the altar upon which her beauty is at once cherished – and sacrificed. It is a long way from Mary Pickford and Theda Bara to Nastassia Kinski, yet it is not all that far in terms of emotional power – of what millions the world over want and demand from those whom they elevate to godhead.

It is a distance no farther than the length of the prostrate worshipping form of a human being outstretched upon the earth before that which it cannot understand – and yet needs. I quote Frazer's 'The Golden Bough', altering it but slightly for our purpose:

La Reine est morte, vive la reine!
Ave Maria!

Index

Figures in italics refer to illustrations